ALLOWED TO LIVE

Russell Kidman, Ph.D.

Copyright© 2014 Russell Kidman, Ph.D.

Email: fourhg@hotmail.com
Web: www.OperationLibertyMinistry.org

All rights reserved

Printed in the United States of America

ISBN 978-0-9860808-1-4

Publishing and Formatting Assisted by
THE OLD PATHS PUBLICATIONS, Inc.
142 Gold Flume Way
Cleveland, Georgia USA 30528
Web: www.theoldpathspublications.com
Email: TOP@theoldpathspublications.com

FOREWORD

I have known Dr. Russell Kidman for many years. We were introduced first as preachers, second as his pastor and third as his friend. After observing Brother Kidman for many years and thinking about what is his most important characteristic that would help all of us the best phrase would be that Dr. Kidman is Loyal. Allow me to show you, Loyal to God including serving Him, Loyal to his wife including loving her, Loyal to his children including training them, Loyal to his church including worshiping, Loyal to his country including sacrificing for us, Loyal to his friends including being there for them. Dr. Kidman learned as a young preacher it is best to be Loyal in the face of opposition. Loyalty is essential in following Christ. I believe that we learn the most about loyalty when we find someone that we believe to be strong and we look up to and find that their loyalty was not found in them as we thought it to be. John 13:36-38, Peter was that example of what loyalty is not to be and Dr. Kidman is that example of what a loyal Christian and friend should be. May his life and book forever be an example of loyalty to your life. Dr. Russ Kidman, my Friend.

Dr. D. Tim McCoy, Ph.D.

TABLE OF CONTENTS

FOREWORD 3
TABLE OF CONTENTS 5
CHAPTER ONE 7
    Starting With A Bang 7
CHAPTER TWO 17
    Mountain Top Experiences 17
CHAPTER THREE 29
    The Worst Of Times 29
CHAPTER FOUR 53
    Taking Care Of Business 53
CHAPTER FIVE 71
    You're In The Army Now 71
CHAPTER SIX 87
    An Help Meet For Him 87
CHAPTER SEVEN 95
    Battle Ready, Sir 95
CHAPTER EIGHT 109
    Persian Gulf War 109
CHAPTER NINE 119

Finding A Reason 119
CHAPTER TEN **125**
Enter The Ministry 125
CHAPTER ELEVEN **143**
Bible College Is Important 143
CHAPTER TWELVE **153**
Operation Liberty 153
CHAPTER THIRTEEN **177**
Tracts & Other Resources 177
ONE LAST THOUGHT? 178
ABOUT THE AUTHOR **197**

CHAPTER ONE

Starting With A Bang

Perhaps it was the way life began for me. Of course, I don't remember this, but, as just a newborn baby I was borrowed by a missionary couple so they could demonstrate to the Church how the natives from Australia would carry their children. No, I am not saying this is what saved me, but just that I was given to serve the Lord at an early age and perhaps that is why God allowed His protection on my life even when I was not saved or living a good or godly life.

There are so many things that happened early in my life it is a struggle on where to start. Like the time my nephew (less than 2 years younger than myself) split my head open with a garden hoe, or when my brother threw a blunt spear at me because I would not wait for him and hit me in the back of the head. Neither of these events were really life threatening but there are enough that I guess I'll start with the first time I was shot. Yes, SHOT, like with a gun... yeah that's right... now that the shock is over, we can begin.

First I need to set the stage a little bit to explain somewhat the family that I grew up in. I have four older siblings which makes me the youngest of the family. Three of those siblings were from my father's first marriage which ended with his wife passing away. My father, after returning from World War II, married my mother. Soon thereafter my other sibling was born, and then me. I am telling you this simply to make the statement that I have siblings much older than myself and, as I already noted, my nephew was just a little younger than me. Now let's get to the nitty-gritty.

Our parents both worked, so one of our older siblings would usually take care of the two younger ones (my brother and I). Our only sister was already married and living outside of the home and the oldest of the boys was in the military, so that only left one other sibling, who was the youngest of the original three children, to watch us. I can only guess that because this was forced upon him, he would be mean to us most of the time, perhaps hoping that he would be punished and not be allowed to watch us anymore. But it did not work that way. On this particular day, with our older brother watching us, we had been wrestling and just being boys tearing up the living room (sorry Mom). As my next older brother and I fought, our older brother left the room and shortly thereafter called for us to come to him. I was the first to leave the living room and as I stepped into the kitchen I was looking at my older brother as he stood there pointing a twenty-two rifle at me. I froze in place because we had been told so many times by Dad not

CHAPTER 1: STARTING WITH A BANG

to touch his guns because he always kept them loaded. I was nearly seven years old, and could not understand why this was happening, when all of a sudden there was a loud noise and a throbbing sensation along my temple. I did not know I had been shot until my brother (the one who had just shot me) came running shouting, "I'm sorry, I'm sorry, I'm sorry, I didn't mean to, I'm sorry!" The bullet had entered at my front temple and stayed between the skull and my skin for the length of my little head and then exited. I don't remember much of what happened next, only that my brother, the supposed-to-be caretaker, the shooter, threatened me not to tell Dad what had happened. He then cut my hair and said I was to say that he cut me with the clippers while cutting my hair.

When Dad and Mom came home that evening they took one look at me and called my older brother, who had been watching us that day, into the house. Dad immediately started asking him what had happened to me as my older brother gave me that look, you know the one, like he wanted to say to me, "What did you tell them?" He started to spin his story of how he was trying to do Dad a favor by cutting our hair as Dad stood there and patiently listened to him. Dad would ask a question and our older brother would do his best to make the answer fit his story. Finally Dad looked at him and asked one final question. "Why is there a hole in the front door?" Our older brother, who up until that point thought Dad believed his tale, looked at the door and then his head just slumped down. Dad told him that I had not said anything to him but he had noticed the hole in the door when he came home, and then put two and two together once he saw me bandaged up. You see, when I was shot I was standing right in front of the front door of our home. After the bullet left my head it went through our wooden front door and the screen door too. I never had to say a word to Dad because the evidence was there all along, and Dad saw it right away.

I look back on this now and understand that God always notices when we try to cover up our sin. God not only sees what we have done wrong but also lets us try to weave our way out. Then He calmly shows us the evidence against us, convicting us of our sin with His righteousness.

> Numbers 32:23 *"But if ye will not do so, behold, ye have sinned against the LORD: and be sure your sin will find you out."*

There are so many stories to tell, and yet which are the ones that are worth the telling? Although we did not farm ourselves, we lived on a farm out in the country. Where we lived was flat farm land, so in the winter we had to make do, or improvise, in order to

CHAPTER 1: STARTING WITH A BANG

have a good time sledding. Dad decided to make a sled that could be pulled behind the tractor and it would hold at least a dozen or more people at a time. It was made all out of wood with metal strips tacked onto the runners so it would glide easily through the snow. However, we got bored with that setup and took the hood off of the '57 Chevy setting behind the barn and flipped that over, hooking it to the tractor. The problem with it was, when the tractor driver turned quickly, the makeshift sled would go sliding on around and then suddenly snap back in behind the tractor. If you did not hold on tightly, it would throw you with a vengeance, usually tearing some part of your clothes or you would get cut somewhere while flying off.

During the summer our older brothers would invite their friends to bring their motorcycles over to have races on a track they built in a place on our farm we called "The Sand Pit." This was about three acres in the middle of a forty-acre field that was just sand, where nothing would grow. For entertainment they would make my brother or me lie on our back with a two by six board lying across our chest like a ramp. They would impress their friends by driving their bikes over us at increasing speeds. Their friends thought this was funny I guess, but I could only lie there and wonder what would happen if they missed the board.

ALLOWED TO LIVE

One summer my oldest brother came home from the service with some fireworks to shoot off. One of the rockets he lit fell over and chased me across the front yard before it went through my legs and out into the neighbor's field where it exploded. I could fill pages with these types of stories, but I want to keep the focus on the times that I should have been killed, or died, usually due to my, or another person's, ignorance, but God spared me anyway.

The last story of this chapter is one that I share from time to time when I am preaching. You see, I had been sick with death pneumonia and missed a lot of school during the third grade. One of the things that I missed was a field trip to Kellogg, Michigan, where my class visited the Kellogg plant where they made all the cereals. My classmates all got to meet "Tony the Tiger" and I missed it. What a letdown for such a young boy. Once I got better, Mom made arrangements for us to go there as a family, and when they heard of why I had missed the field trip, special arrangements were made for my own time with "Tony The Tiger." Consequently, I received several things that were autographed by him that the other kids did not get. This made the trip extra special for me because, like I said, I had almost died that spring from pneumonia.

The real story here though is what happened the

CHAPTER 1: STARTING WITH A BANG

day before we went into the Kellogg factory. Mom made a big deal out of our trip and, even though we could have traveled there and back in one day, she got us a motel room just down the road from the factory and we stayed there the night before our tour of the factory. While we were there I asked Mom if I could go swimming in their pool to which she replied, "Of course." So Mom, my brother, and I headed down to the pool to go swimming. There were not a lot of people staying at the motel that night, so there were only the three of us and two other people at the pool while we were there. The other two people were a mother and daughter who were traveling together and the daughter was in her late teen years. I was only eight years old and my brother would have been ten. He had a pair of underwater goggles with him but he was not using them, so I put them on and did some diving around the pool. When he saw that I had his goggles on, he got upset and grabbed them as I swam by. Well, they did not come off my head but they did come off my face and filled with water. As I came to the surface to get a breath of air the water from inside the goggles ran down my face and I was unable to get any air. Unable to tread water, and being in the deep end of the pool, I sank back under the water as the goggles filled up with water again. From the bottom of the pool I pushed with all my might towards the surface, and, as I broke through, gasping for air, again water from the goggles came plunging down across my face and into my mouth, preventing me from getting a breath. I am not sure how many times this took place but I know that I was about to give up as I could not seem to get a breath and was already in a panic mode. Although all I had to do was remove the goggles from my head and I could have gotten the air I needed, when you are eight years old and in a panic, you don't think right; you just want air. As I slumped under the water again, and just as everything began to go black, that teenage girl dove into the pool and pulled me out, placing me on the side of the pool. She ripped the goggles from my head and tossed them away as she did what she could to save my life.

I do not have a clue who this girl was or even if she would remember saving a poor boy in a pool in Kellogg, Michigan back in nineteen sixty-eight. That day God used her to give me life for another day. I tell this story over and over because it is like the salvation of God by grace through His Son, Jesus Christ. I was nothing to her, but in my wretched state drowning, she took pity on me and saved my life. Isn't that what God has done for us too? He saw us drowning in sin and despair and through His grace he saved us for His glory! What a picture of salvation, unmerited favor, grace and mercy! I have never forgotten the kindness of this stranger and hope to one day meet her again. So

CHAPTER 1: STARTING WITH A BANG

until that day happens, whoever you are, THANK YOU for saving my life that day!

> John 3:16-21 *"For God so loved the world, that he gave his only begotten Son, that whosoever believeth in him should not perish, but have everlasting life. (17) For God sent not his Son into the world to condemn the world; but that the world through him might be saved. (18) He that believeth on him is not condemned: but he that believeth not is condemned already, because he hath not believed in the name of the only begotten Son of God. (19) And this is the condemnation, that light is come into the world, and men loved darkness rather than light, because their deeds were evil. (20) For every one that doeth evil hateth the light, neither cometh to the light, lest his deeds should be reproved. (21) But he that doeth truth cometh to the light, that his deeds may be made manifest, that they are wrought in God."*

Please do not take these stories as a complaint against my older brothers; it is simply my desire that you see God's hand of protection.

> Genesis 50:20 *"But as for you, ye thought evil against me; but God meant it unto good, to*

ALLOWED TO LIVE

bring to pass, as it is this day, to save much people alive."

CHAPTER TWO
Mountain Top Experiences

Many changes have now taken place since the ending of chapter one. My parents were now divorced and both remarried. Where we had grown up was now a distant memory long gone. Our new step-dad worked for the Bureau of Indian Affairs and after marrying our mother he moved us to an Indian reservation in New Mexico. The overall experience of living on an Indian reservation was very educating, although it was also one of the most trying times of our lives.

My family heritage comes from immigrants who came from England five generations before me. I mention this because that makes me an Anglo-Saxon, or as most in America like to call us, "The White Man." Being "white" and living on an Indian reservation meant that one of the first things I learned there was what it means to experience racism. Simply because I was "white" I was hated by the Indians with whom we lived, went to school, and played. For the nearly three years that we lived on that reservation I was forced to fight, or I was jumped, almost every day of my life.

Beating after beating took place and with each beating I learned how to fight. I also learned how to hate, which replaced the love of God I had always known before. I learned to mistrust everyone; hate first and ask questions later. The Indians hated me not only because I was "white," but because our new step-dad was in charge of the dormitory life of all the kids that were bused in from the reservation during the school year and put up in dormitories. This was necessary because of us being seven thousand feet up in the mountains and in the winter it would snow nearly every day. The other reason was because the reservation was nearly one hundred and eighty miles long. To run a daily route would take up to six hours just to pick up all the students and then another six hours to take them home. I am sure you can see how this would be impossible.

With everyone put up in dorms in the small town where the school was, there was no need to run buses. Therefore, no matter how much it snowed, we had school because we all lived and walked less than a mile to school. It was usually as I was walking home that I would get jumped, fighting off one, two, or more as they simply wanted to just beat me to a pulp. There's one time in particular that I remember, which took place the last year we lived there. I was on my way home and was jumped by two eighteen-year-old seniors from the small school. As I was wrestling to get away from them, I noticed a board lying on the

CHAPTER 2: MOUNTAIN TOP EXPERIENCES

ground with two sixteen-penny spikes sticking all the way through. I picked up the board and began swinging it as a weapon. I can remember them laughing at me as I tried to defend myself, that is until I planted that board and the two nails into one of their backsides. As that one whimpered away in pain the second one had second thoughts about finishing me off. Just as I thought he might leave me alone he grabbed me and, well, you can guess what I did. Let's just say for the record that he whimpered away too! One of the reasons I say that living on that reservation was educating is because when I arrived there I was a coward, but when I left there I was not afraid to stand up for myself.

While living there my brother and I got into mountain climbing and camping. Because of the hatred towards us we would escape to the mountain peaks during the summer months. Once it was warm enough we would pack our backpacks on Thursday evenings and as soon as we got home from school on Friday we would put our packs on and head for the mountain tops. The only rule was that we had to be back in time to get ready for Church on Sunday. During the summer we would go up on the mountain tops for days on end, only coming down to get more food and supplies. It was a great place to get away to, and not for the faint of heart either. Once we got used to the thin air from being in high altitudes it still took us over two hours of steady climbing to get to our favorite camping site. From there we could see the whole town below and even the front door of our house. If the porch light was turned on it meant that we were needed at home and we would make the trip back down the mountain.

You see the town we lived in was surrounded by two mountain ranges. It was widely known that mountain lions had been spotted on the southern range, but they seemed to stay off the northern range. No one knew why this was, but at least it allowed us to camp and explore the northern range. It was during one of these week-long trips that we had an adventure most people find hard to believe. This particular week we had gone up on the mountain top and pitched our tent on ground that was shale stone. That means that you could not drive a stake into the ground because the ground would just flake apart and the stake would not go into the ground. In order to put up our tent we picked a spot that had bushes at a close distance to both sides of the tent and tied ropes from the bushes to the tent to hold it up. It did not look pretty but at least it worked and kept the tent up. After exploring, playing, and just enjoying the evening, we turned into the tent and called it a night. Early in the morning as we awoke from a restful night's sleep we found that one end of

CHAPTER 2: MOUNTAIN TOP EXPERIENCES

the tent was lying on my face. I grabbed the tent pole and pushed the tent back up into place and noticed right away that I could see daylight through the sides and top of the tent. I called to my brother as he replied, "Yeah I see it, I see it!" There were long gashes across the sides of the tent and several near the top of the tent too. We crawled out and began to survey the area around our camp. Immediately I noticed that most of our ropes had been cut with something very sharp. My first thought was that someone had come up on the mountain top that night and cut up my tent just to be mean. That is when I noticed the ground around the tent. Yes, you guessed it! The mountain lion had come up on the northern range and got tangled in our tent as it came through. I can only imagine that it struggled to get free from the ropes and in doing so tore into the sides of our tent, slicing the ropes into pieces, and then ran off. Why we did not hear this huge cat ripping the tent apart or why it did not attack us further I'll never know, but it happened anyway.

Then there was another time when some of our cousins arrived during the night and they were amazed the next morning at how close the mountain peaks were to our house. After a little prodding we talked them into a "day climb." That means that we would climb as far as we could for about four hours and then regardless of how far we made it we would start back home. Well, we made it to the highest peak in less than three hours that day. Knowing it would only take about two hours to get back down we stayed up there a little longer than we had planned.

There was a rock formation on that mountain peak that looked like the "Peanuts" character, "Snoopy." As we walked across the top of "Snoopy's" head, our hair began to stand up on end. One of our cousins had hair down to the bottom of her back and it stood completely straight up into the air. Living on an Indian reservation we tried to fit in with the Indians and had grown our hair long down to the middle of our backs and it also stood straight up into the air. From atop the mountain we could see for miles and miles. Off in the distance we saw a thunderstorm come up over the horizon, and figured we were standing at a magnetically charged point on the earth's crust. We decided we had better get back down off that mountain as soon as possible.

After climbing down as quickly as we could, and once able to, we began to run for the house. With just a couple hundred feet to go it began to rain and was in a full downpour by the time we made it to the house. It was already late into the evening and as night fell the storm became worse and worse. Lightning bolts were flashing with a vengeance all through the night, some so loud that it would make your hair curl

CHAPTER 2: MOUNTAIN TOP EXPERIENCES

(figuratively of course). In the morning when we looked out the front window of our house, "Snoopy" was missing half of his face and one ear. We all stood there in shock because we then realized the power of the magnetic currents flowing in and out of our planet. In this case they were flowing out like a giant lightning rod just waiting for that storm to arrive. Who knows what would have happened if we had not made it down from off the mountain that day.

Ok, one more mountain story and we will move on. This one takes place just a few days after the lightning storm as three of us decided to go back up on the mountain top and see what it looked like from up there. Once on top it was amazing the damage from the lightning strikes and shocking as we looked at where we had been standing a couple of days prior. The top of the mountain was covered with charred marks from where the lightning had struck over and over. The actual spot where we had been standing was no longer there but now a sheer drop off of a cliff was all that remained.

Our cousin wanted to explore the whole mountain range and we went with him for a while but soon we had had enough. That is when my brother and I decided to find another way down the mountain from where we were instead of back-tracking to the way we came up. This meant exploring, which was exciting to me, so off we went heading down the mountain, leaving our cousin to go on by himself. The terrain was kind of steep but still easily passable at first. Then it got even steeper still. This should have been a hint to what we were getting ourselves into, but we were young and "EXPLORERS." Before I knew where we were, we had found a "rock slide." Ok, let me define what I mean by this because I am sure you're already thinking of a bunch of rocks falling and sliding down the face of the mountain. No, that is not what I mean. This "rock slide" was a large, rather smooth rock that was like a slide from your local recreation park or playground. My brother went first and when he reached the bottom he shouted with glee that it was at least twenty-five feet long and how much fun it was sliding down it. So I sat down on it and pushed off for a quick but exciting ride down this natural slide where I joined my brother waiting at the bottom. After whooping and hollering for a spell at what a great time that was, we looked for a way to go back up and do it again. That is when we noticed that there was not a way back up and that we were stuck on a ledge with nothing but a cliff below us.

   We searched the ledge heading west first and found that it ended up against a large rock that we could not climb. We then set out to search the ledge in the other direction and found a trail heading east so we followed

CHAPTER 2: MOUNTAIN TOP EXPERIENCES

it that way. For a while I thought everything was going to be all right, but that illusion soon came to an end. As we traveled along this ledge, which was quite wide at first, it began to get narrower; the further we went along the narrower it became. If that was not bad enough, it also began to tilt towards the one or two-hundred-foot cliff that kept us from going down any further. By now the other side of the ledge was also a sheer cliff that we still could not climb, so our only choice was to keep going along the ledge we were on. The good news was that the ledge was still at least five or six feet wide, so as long as we stayed close to the wall we felt safe enough to continue.

However, this good news did not last very long as the ledge again began to get even narrower and tilting ever more towards the edge of the cliff. If that were not bad enough, the ledge was made out of "shale rock." Remember the stuff that brakes off easily that we could not drive our stakes into? Yeah, that stuff. Each and every step had to be planned as we clung to the wall with all our might. I was so scared at this point and voiced my fears to my brother. He would try to encourage me, but little did I know he was having the same fears that we would never make it off that ledge alive. Moving inches would take fifteen minutes or more, moving feet took hours. It was hot, probably about one hundred fourteen degrees or so, and we became very weary and thirsty and weak. After about four and a half hours of being scared out of our minds, clinging, slipping and barely grabbing hold of something to stop our fall, we finally noticed that the ledge was getting wider again as it began to level off too.

That is when to my wondering eyes did appear... no, it was not Santa or his reindeer but a yucca plant. Yes, a yucca plant, and not just any yucca plant but one that was very familiar to us. You see, to get to the top of the mountain you had to go through a crevasse, or some even called it a cave, and just before you got to that crevasse there was a huge yucca plant. Never had I seen much beauty in that plant before, but today it was the most beautiful plant I had ever seen. We looked at the plant and then at each other and began to cry as we knew we had made it across the ledge and now knew our way home.

We were exhausted, so it took a little longer than usual to climb down the now familiar part of the mountain as we headed for home. The walk back to the house from the base of the mountain seemed twice as far, but, we had made it. We were alive! We opened the front door and entered the house to find our cousin sitting there in the living room with one question for us. He asked, "Are you just getting home?" He went on to tell us that he had been home for hours and

CHAPTER 2: MOUNTAIN TOP EXPERIENCES

wondered where we had gone. As we began to tell him what had happened, our mother came into the room, catching just a few words about us being on the mountain. Right away she asked us if we had seen or run into the two idiots that were on the face of the cliff all afternoon. Maybe it was the look on our faces or perhaps we uttered something without realizing it but that is when she realized her two sons had been the idiots.

How do you punish children who have just stood on the edge of Hell and lived to tell about it? I don't know about my brother but I was not saved at this point in my life, so had I fallen, it would have not only been to my death but to eternal death. We were then lectured on the gravity (no pun intended) of the situation and had to promise that we would not try that again.

Isaiah 40:29-31 *"He giveth power to the faint; and to them that have no might he increaseth strength. Even the youths shall faint and be weary, and the young men shall utterly fall: But they that wait upon the LORD shall renew their strength; they shall mount up with wings as eagles; they shall run, and not be weary; and they shall walk, and not faint."*

CHAPTER THREE

The Worst Of Times

Let me start this chapter by first saying that the following stories are from my teenage years and will portray probably the saddest part of my life. They are not meant to justify or glorify sin but to show that God loves sinners, even those who make bad choices.

I was no angel, that is for sure, but there were things that had happened which contributed to this pathetic attitude I had as a teenager. While we lived in New Mexico with our Mother and step-dad we learned not only the hate from the Indians but what it was like to be hated just for being alive. To say that our step-dad did not like children would be an understatement at best. Why he wanted to marry our mother was what I could never figure out because he knew he would have to take us with her. A child needs correction when they are wrong but they should not be required to live in absolute fear. During those years living out west we had been beaten by our step-dad with most items which were in a typical home of the nineteen seventies. My brother was taken to the "clinic" twice with his skull split open and a broken arm. Although I was never taken to the "clinic" or hospital because of the beatings I received, there were health issues that would plague me for years to come.

During the summer of nineteen seventy-four we took our step-dad to court after telling our real dad what had been happening to us for the last three years. It was a long and drawn out process which came down to if we were lying or if our step-dad was lying. All I know for sure is that our mother had been putting money away for our college educations for years because this was important to her. Instead of the case being about how we had been abused by our step-dad it somehow got turned into whether or not our real father was fit to take custody of us. Lies were told about our real dad and the college money all disappeared. You can read into that whatever you want but the end result was that we were sent back into the home of our mother and her husband who could not wait to take vengeance on us for dragging him through the courts. What was a bad place to live became a nightmare for my brother and me as once again the beatings began.

When children are raised in this environment, they tend to not want to spend any more time at "home" than they need to. The one victory from the court case was that our mother had to move back to within five hundred miles of our father, and that we did. We moved to a small town in Ohio and tried to make new friends, but no sooner would we get started in a school

CHAPTER 3: THE WORST OF TIMES

and we would have to move again. This happened several times before we finally stayed in one place, but the effects of continually moving took its toll. Being new in town, it is not always easy to make friends, so when someone showed themselves friendly we were open to it. However, these friends began to lead us down paths that caused further dissention between us and our mother let alone our step-dad.

My brother began hanging out with a family that was involved in the drug world and it was not long before he was using drugs. I lasted a little bit longer but ended up getting into drugs myself because of the kids I chose to hang out with. What drew me into this world was not the "getting high" part of it but the money that could be made by selling it for my supplier. I had a part-time job too, so Mom never questioned all the money I seemed to have, but God was about to reveal to her what was going on. When I turned sixteen I got my driver's license and bought a car to get around in. One fall day my brother and I, along with several of our friends, decided to go hunting for rabbits. We all loaded up in my car and drove out to a hedgerow where we had hunted before. I loaded my shotgun and headed into the woods ahead of everyone else. I was supposed to find a good spot and they would begin to walk through the woods from the south to drive the rabbits toward me. The next thing I remember is hearing a loud noise and the sound of shot pellets rushing through the trees. I spun in place turning my back to the sound just in time as I was hit in the back, knocking me flat on the ground. I don't know how long I was unconscious but when I awoke several of my friends were leaning over me shouting at me asking if I was all right. Two of our friends and my brother took off in the direction I said the sound came from to see who had shot me. Yes, this was the second time I had been shot, and again God provided the protection necessary for my life to continue. I had on a Vietnam era army jacket that had been given to me just a few days before this happened. Between that and all the foliage, the shot that traveled through it slowed down enough that it did not penetrate through the coat other than to leave deep indentations in my back. Although there was no blood, it felt like I had been kicked by two Kentucky mules at the same time, knocking the wind out of me and leaving me unconscious. We did not get any rabbits.

This is where it gets a little ugly. One night my brother and I picked up a mutual friend and partied the night away. The town we lived in had just instituted a new curfew that anyone under the age of eighteen could not be on the streets after ten o'clock at night. We had been out in the country partying when one of the other two suggested that we go back into town for

CHAPTER 3: THE WORST OF TIMES

a while. We were all impaired and under age for the curfew, so when we saw a police officer cruising where we were parked, I panicked and took off trying to outrun the police. You've watched "Cops," right? Yeah, that's exactly what happened. We got caught and taken to jail for the night. Mom came and bailed us out and as we were walking out to the car she got my attention without saying one word. Now you must understand that my mother was six feet tall and was a healthy woman to say the least. She swung from her heels with everything she had and caught me along the side of my head, spinning me on my heels. As the car we were walking by went past me for the third time, I jumped for it to stop the spinning. In all the fights I've ever been in during my life, I've never been hit like that and did not ever want to experience it again. The next day I sold all my drugs and never used, sold, or participated in any illegal drugs again! EVER!

While involved in this illegal world of trafficking and using drugs I was often placed in a position which, shall we say, was threatening to my life. There were always lots of guys with guns at the drug house where I would pick up my supplies. There was always the threat of the "cops" finding out about you and dragging you off to jail. But the worst threat was when you found out that you were selling in a rival group's area and they did not take this very lightly. There were at least three times that I had a gun placed up against my skull as I was educated in these matters or escorted out of that particular part of town. This is the side of the "drug world" most people don't find out about until it is too late and they become plant food, daisy fertilizer; you know, DEAD!

Although I had turned my back on the "illegal drug world," things did not get better because I went from illegal drugs to one that has been legal in America for over one hundred years; alcohol. Shortly after this event my step-dad gave me the last beating by him that I would take. This time when the beating began I stood up and said, "NO!" I raised my fists toward him and watched as he backed away with a shocked look on his face. He turned and walked out of the room and then left the house. Four days later he came up to me and said, "You know the two of us cannot live in this house together" to which I replied, "I know...GOOD-BYE!" Two days later, while we were gone with Mom to a family get-together, he moved out and left my mother. My brother and I, along with the help of our friends, would follow him with our cars to harass him, because we found out that he was having an affair on our mother. It got so bad that he went into hiding and no one would let me know where he had gone. Again this is how God protected me because the HATE I had for him was so powerful that I would have killed him with

CHAPTER 3: THE WORST OF TIMES

no remorse if I could have found him.

Mom was not very happy and blamed me for running him out of the house. So that summer she moved back to Michigan where she had a house she still owned from before they had married. I begged her to stay in Ohio at least until I finished school, but she was so upset that she just left. I had to make a decision. Should I move again with Mom or stay in the school where I was getting good grades and had some better friends? It was mostly about staying in a school that I liked that made me choose to stay. My mother was not in favor of it, but she did not make a fuss about it either. Our mother had ignored the fact that her husband was beating her children, which led to the breakup of her marriage. These two things started a rift between my mother and I that grew deeper year after year until we would hardly speak to one another. It was not until I was in my twenties that we sat down one day and talked it all out. As of the writing of this book, I can say that from that time on I did all I could to help my mother up until her passing on to glory in February of two thousand and eight. Life got even tougher for me after Mom left. It was just a month before my seventeenth birthday, but before I go on with my story I want you, the reader, to know this simple fact; what pride tore apart, God restored by grace!

The dream of most rebellious teenagers is to be on

their own, but if they only knew what this meant, I am convinced that they would also second guess such a desire. I lived that so-called dream, and here is how it went. My girlfriend's aunt agreed to rent me a room, but there were conditions. I had to be in the house by six o'clock in the evening and in bed by eight. I had to buy and maintain my own food supply but not take up any room in their cupboards or fridge. I could only take a bath before seven o'clock in the evening because they did not want to hear the water draining after that. I was never given a key to the house, so when I would come home late I would be locked out for the night. YEAH, you guessed it… that did not work out for very long. One evening as I came to the house I saw my luggage setting on the porch with no explanation. But none was really needed as I was ready to leave anyway.

For the next year I actually lived with my girlfriend's dad. Her parents had divorced so she moved in with her mother to keep things proper. The rules for my new arrangement were that I would look after the younger children while he was at work and do my best to keep the house kept up. Again I had to keep my own food tucked away in my room but other than that I had the run of the house. I was a help to him, the kids both liked me a lot anyway, and I had a warm place to live. Why did this only last for a year?

CHAPTER 3: THE WORST OF TIMES

Because it became an uncomfortable place to live once his daughter and I broke up and she brought her new boyfriend home to meet Dad. Once again I had to look for a place to live.

This time was different, as I had no place to go, and after repeatedly imposing on several friends, their parents did not want me coming over any more. I spent that winter living in my car which was a Mustang II. I am over six feet tall and lived in a little bitty Mustang, and it was not pretty either. I would sleep in a down sleeping bag with the front seats folded down so I could stretch out my legs and be able to reach the starter to get some heat in there in the mornings before I got up. I would get to school early so I could grab a shower in the gym before classes started. I did any and all odd jobs I could to earn money to buy gas for the car and food to eat. I had to stay out of trouble as I could not afford for the authorities to find out that as an under-age teenager, I was living on my own. I delivered pizza and newspapers, cleaned houses and gas station bathrooms, and anything else that was legal to earn money. Yes, I would still party, but only with close friends who I knew would protect me. Well, at least from the authorities anyway.

At one of these friend's houses we had a huge party because his parents were going to be out of town for the whole weekend. The booze we went through that weekend was astronomical and to the best of my knowledge there were over two hundred people who attended that party that Friday night after the football game. I had just broken up with my girlfriend whom I had dated for four years and was devastated.

If you would like a word of advice right here it would be this: Be friends with everyone, but give your heart to no one until God shows you the person He wants you with forever.

> Mat 6:31-34 *"Therefore take no thought, saying, What shall we eat? or, What shall we drink? or, Wherewithal shall we be clothed? (32) (For after all these things do the Gentiles seek:) for your heavenly Father knoweth that ye have need of all these things. (33) But seek ye first the kingdom of God, and his righteousness; and all these things shall be added unto you. (34) Take therefore no thought for the morrow: for the morrow shall take thought for the things of itself. Sufficient unto the day is the evil thereof."*

I was ready to tie one on and forget my troubles and that is just what I did. The list of what I drank that night is not what is important but that in the spirit of having a good time and drowning my sorrows, I nearly died of alcohol poisoning. I had so much liquor in my

CHAPTER 3: THE WORST OF TIMES

system that I passed out sitting in a chair with my head leaned backwards up against the wall in the kitchen. My "wonderful friend," who was throwing the party, saw me there and decided for me that I needed a shot of whisky. So he poured the rest of a half-gallon down my open throat. I do not remember much from that night, but I was told that I beat the living thunder out of a guy I did not like, and was placed outside in the backseat of a car where I heaved all night long, filling the floor boards with vomit. When I think about that evening, what could have happened, and what happened thereafter, there is a passage of Scripture that always comes to mind:

> Proverbs 23:30-35 *"They that tarry long at the wine; they that go to seek mixed wine. Look not thou upon the wine when it is red, when it giveth his colour in the cup, when it moveth itself aright. At the last it biteth like a serpent, and stingeth like an adder. Thine eyes shall behold strange women, and thine heart shall utter perverse things. Yea, thou shalt be as he that lieth down in the midst of the sea, or as he that lieth upon the top of a mast. <u>They have stricken me, shalt thou say, and I was not sick; they have beaten me, and I felt it not: when shall I awake? I will seek it yet again.</u>"*
>
> THIS IS SO TRUE!

This was not the last time I drank or tied one on; that would come years down the road. The wisdom of years now allows me to understand how close I was that night to going out into eternity drunk, lost, and headed for Hell! With all that booze in me I bet I would have really burnt well in that fiery pit! Since our flesh is not consumed in Hell's fire, perhaps also the alcohol would only intensify the flames of our mortal doom. This is not theology but just a simple thought I had while writing this book.

I've written a Gospel Tract called "One Last Thought" that is about the next story from my life. Here is an excerpt from that tract about the day my eyes were opened and I realized my need of a Saviour.

My car by now had about run its course and was fast on its way to the grave. I needed another form of transportation. A car was out of the question because I could not afford the payments for anything which was reliable. I had always wanted a motorcycle and found out that I could get one for only a fourth of my income. So I did. It was a beautiful 750 Four CBK to say the least. With a four-cylinder engine bolted beneath your legs, and only about 500 lbs. of bike weight to push, YEAH IT WAS FAST! In a very short time I was riding this bike just like the pros you see on TV. I could lay her down in a corner as good as the best of them, and even chased down a Ferrari; well, for

CHAPTER 3: THE WORST OF TIMES

a little ways anyway.

I was now eighteen years old, strong, healthy, a senior in high school and would be graduating in just a little over two months. I had a "new ride," and was on my way to take my "new girl" out for the evening. About halfway there I realized I had forgotten the ring she had given me, so I went back to get it. As I was leaving town the second time there was a very slow car in front of me, so I whipped my bike right on around them. I was now going about 50-mph, and as I was passing them a semi-truck pulled out onto the road heading the same direction. He was moving slow so I decided to pass him too. As I began to pass this big truck, he decided to turn left, again crossing my path of travel, as he turned into a local restaurant. The witnesses say that I jumped 20 feet into the air, over the truck, and tumbled to where I lay bleeding profusely. In just a fraction of a second my bike smashed into the truck.

ALLOWED TO LIVE

Although brought up in Church, taught about Christ as a child, even baptized at age 14, my last conscious thought was:

I'M GOING TO HELL!!

At that moment I KNEW without a doubt that
GOD was real,
    Death was real,
        Hell was real,
And I was going to split it wide open.

A copy of this tract is included in the back of the book. Additional copies of the tract may be reproduced as needed.

I have to tell you about the injuries from this accident. The odds are astronomical of surviving an accident between a motorcycle and a semi. Add to this the fact that I was not wearing a helmet and the odds become nearly impossible. There was a ninety-nine percent chance that I should have been killed that day,

CHAPTER 3: THE WORST OF TIMES

but that did not happen. Out of the one percent that is left there was a ninety-five percent chance that I should have been left a vegetable for the rest of my life, but that did not happen. Taking the remaining five percent of the first one percent, there was less than a three percent chance that I would have no major injuries at all.

Six days after the accident happened I walked out of the hospital with the following injuries: I had a nine-inch laceration across the left side of my head and no concussion. I had a laceration in the shape of the letter "C" on my left knee. Other than that, just some road rash burns on my arms and legs, and that was it. What blew my mind was when I went to leave the hospital they handed me my pants from the day of the accident. The cut on my left knee in the shape of the letter "C" was directly under a tear in my pants in the shape of a cross. What I saw was Christ on the Cross and it scared me so much that, suffice it to say, I did not sleep much until I finally gave in and got saved. However this did not take place for over another year. God will get our attention, but how far he has to go and at what cost to our physical body remains up to us and when we will pay attention to God.

I have to add in here, and do a little back tracking, as I also wanted to mention the three times I was stabbed. The first one happened when we lived out in

New Mexico and was simply a sledding accident. One of the boys had a runner sled that the runners did not curl up on the back end but simply were cut off diagonally, leaving them as sharp points. I took off down the mountain where we would go sledding, riding on a saucer, and he came flying by me about half way down the hill. At the very bottom was a little bump that we had worn the snow off of as it was beginning to warm up. When the other boy hit that spot, his sled stopped on the spot leaving the back ends of the runners pointed up into the air. If you have ever ridden on a saucer, you know that you always go down backwards and so I never saw it coming until I was impaled upon the back of his sled. Several boys helped me get back home, and it took a couple of stitches, but there were no internal injuries. What puzzled me about the incident is that I had on a one-piece snow suit and there was not even a scratch on it, let alone a hole. There was a hole in my shirt and T-shirt but not in my snow suit. I have never been able to wrap my head around that one other than to say, only God knows for sure.

The second time I got stabbed was during a fight at school. The only reason that I even mention it is because at that time there was a huge push to get rid of anything that had lead in it, such as paint, gasoline, pencils etc... Well, the fight took place during the first

CHAPTER 3: THE WORST OF TIMES

school we were placed in when we first moved to Ohio. The boy that I was fighting picked up a pencil that had been knocked to the floor and stabbed me in the leg with it. It penetrated down to the bone and stopped as he broke it off. That just made me madder than I already was. Yes, I won the fight and then pulled the pencil out of my leg, got a bandage, and went on with my life. There were no teachers or adults in the room when the fight took place and I never told anyone about it until years later, after I was grown. I just went home and kept pouring peroxide on it until it healed.

The third and hopefully last time I was stabbed also happened during a fight. Except this time the fight was with my brother who was just twenty months older than myself. We were in my bedroom acting like normal brothers act. Yes, we were arguing. I had a bowie knife that I had purchased for hunting laying on my dresser and as we started to fight my brother grabbed the knife, pulling it out of the sheath and brandishing it about in front of my face. Finally he raised it above his head and brought it down toward me like he intended to stab me in the chest. I put my left arm up in the path of the knife and allowed him to stab my arm instead of my chest. While he was distracted with the knife being in my arm, I hauled off and let him have a good right uppercut, knocking him out and stopping the threat to my life. Again I did not make a big deal out of the wound to my arm but took a butterfly bandage out of the first aid kit we kept in our home and placed it over the wound. Then I wrapped it with gauze and an ace bandage. When my mother asked why I was wearing an ace bandage I just told her I had hurt my arm and it helped it to feel better. I was after all somewhat of the athletic type, so she accepted that excuse, and like before, I would clean the wound every day with peroxide and re-bandage it until it healed completely.

This now leads to the third time I was shot. Yes, I was shot again. We were at my grandfather's farm and my girlfriend was with me. I was showing her around the farm, going from building to building and telling her what each building was used for. We had just entered the big barn where the hay was stored up in the lofts and the cattle were kept down in the lower parts. There was another huge lean-to shed that came off the big barn and that is where grandpa kept his combine and other large implements. That part of the barn had two large doors so the equipment could be driven in one side and out the other. As we walked down into this part of the barn, my brother stepped into the opposite doorway and had an arrow loaded into his bow, ready to shoot. He was mad at me for who knows what, and had the arrow pointed right at my girlfriend and me. We shouted back and forth at each other

CHAPTER 3: THE WORST OF TIMES

several times until, all of a sudden, the arrow came rushing towards us and stuck in my left hand. It is important to understand where my hand was when it was hit by the arrow. I had my arm around my girlfriend and my hand was just about over her left kidney. Had my hand not been there, the arrow could have done a lot of damage to her as it would have pierced her kidney for sure. The only reason it stopped when it hit my hand is because it hit right on top of the main bone in my hand, but with enough force that it left an impression of my hand on her body through her clothing. As soon as he saw what he had done he ran towards the house, I guess to make up a story of why I was chasing him, but once Grandma and Mom saw my hand bleeding, they knew there was more to the story than what he was telling them. That is when I had to spill the beans on what had happened and, boy, did he get it; and lost his bow and arrows too. You know when I tell people that I have been shot three times they automatically assume that it must have been while I was serving in the army during Desert Storm, but NO! Two out of three times that I have been shot was by FAMILY! And although I never found out who the other person was that shot me, I have always had my suspicions that it might have been my step-dad, which would make it three for three, but that is only a suspicion.

Let's now jump back to where we were before and talk about the cars, speed, and stupidity. My first car was a piece of junk Camaro. I just had to have it and talked Mom into buying it for me. It had a three twenty-seven Chevy short block engine with a three quarter racing cam which made it kind of quick. Other than that the body was rusted badly, to be kind, and it had a "Fred Flintstone" floor in it. I was offered double what I had paid for it two days after I bought it and should have sold it, but NO! Instead I drove it like a race car and could not understand why I always had to fix things in it, especially the electrical system. I went through more alternators in one month than most parts stores were selling in the same time frame. But I was sixteen and had a Camaro and drove like an idiot! It wasn't very long before I blew the engine up and was fortunate to find someone who was willing to give me a hundred dollars for it.

My next car I purchased from my mother. She had bought it brand new and it was now five years old. When she bought the car she was told by the salesman that the car was manufactured as a police patrol car but they had filled their quota, so they just painted it green and sold it as a regular passenger car. It wasn't the prettiest car one had ever seen, but it was fast and solidly built for high speed chases. Not really the car a teenage boy should have, but I did. I called it "The

CHAPTER 3: THE WORST OF TIMES

Sleeper" because it was a little banged up and did not look like much from the outside, but with it being set-up as a police cruiser, I could lure other guys with hot cars to race against the old clunker, and then I would smoke them with its hidden treasures. It was not very long before I had a reputation, and there was always someone there to challenge it. We would go out into the country on some new, or at least, smoothly paved road, and put our skills to the test. Many of those races I won, not because I had the faster car, but because (as I thought back then) I had nerves of steel. The TRUTH be known, I was just plain stupid and drove with reckless abandonment.

The last car of my teen years was the Mustang that I have already mentioned earlier in this chapter. It was four years old when I bought it and after doing just a little customizing inside the car, it was a nice ride. Several of my friends wanted to buy it from me but I would not sell. Well, at least until I ran it into the ground from driving it with no water in the radiator. It still ran after that but not the same as it had before. I hesitate to mention all the things I did in these cars, and if you are a youngster, a teenager, or a grown person who just never grew up, let me say this to you. Any idiot can drive reckless, but it takes an intelligent person to realize that driving a car takes responsibility. We fail to realize that a car is simply a large weapon that we take possession of to handle. When we drive recklessly we often lose control of this beast, which then turns on us and devours us, our friends, and sometimes other innocent victims who get in our path. Too many of our young people today are dying behind the wheel of their car simply because they feel they have to prove what a talented driver they are. If you want to prove your talent behind the wheel of a car, then go to a race track and do it. At best you will only kill yourself and not some innocent bystander or the person who just happened to be driving by!

August tenth, nineteen seventy-eight. What about it you ask? That is the day our class is remembered for. The class I graduated from high school with is remembered as the class of death. We had so many people die or get killed during our four years of high school that we have been given that tag. August tenth of nineteen seventy-eight was our first football game of the season. Yes it was early in the year as school had not even started yet and we were already playing our first football game. Many of our class saw this as an infringement on their summer vacation and refused to attend the game that night. There were football players, band players, cheerleaders, and just classmates who did not show up for the game. For those who did not show up, here is a listing of some of what happened that night:

CHAPTER 3: THE WORST OF TIMES

Two brothers who were both on the football team, and three girls, were all out partying in the one boy's car. Two of the girls were cheerleaders and the other one just a classmate along for the ride. After several hours of partying they dropped the one girl off at home and then just a few miles down the road crashed their car into a telephone pole, clipping it off fifty feet in the air. The car was twisted so that if the front tires were on the ground, the back tires would be pointing up into the air. None of the passengers of that car had on their seat belts and the girl in the front seat went through the front window up to her shoulders, decapitating her head as it rolled away from the crumpled wreck. One of the boys is in a wheelchair to this day, and the other one had a broken nose. The girl who had been riding in the back seat had just some slight injuries and recovered fine. However, the girl they dropped off just a few minutes prior to the accident went crazy because she had been sitting in the front seat just minutes before and that could have been her.

One of our band members stayed home and was cleaning his dad's revolver when it went off, shooting him in the leg. He was rushed to the hospital with just a few tendons still attached and holding the remains of his leg to the rest of his body. After many surgeries and months upon months of rehabilitation, he was finally able to walk again but with a definite limp.

ALLOWED TO LIVE

Another one of our band members had enough of life that night and placed the barrel of a revolver in his mouth and pulled the trigger. Yet another one of our band members was out on a date with her new boyfriend and they had been drinking. He lost control of his car as he sped around a sharp curve and smashed into a concrete abutment, killing the driver and making a vegetable out of the girl. Still another classmate, who was in the Occupational Work Experience program at school which helped you get a job and support yourself while attending school, had just been hired at a local factory and used his new paycheck as a down payment on a brand new van. He was going to get insurance on it with the next pay check (you did not need insurance to purchase back then), but he got drunk that night and rolled the van five times totaling it and putting himself in the hospital on life support. The list goes on with more suicides and careless accidents that took the lives of so many that one night in August. Kind of makes you think of what is said in the Scriptures:

Numbers 32:23 *"But if ye will not do so, behold, ye have sinned against the LORD: and be sure your sin will find you out."*

CHAPTER FOUR

Taking Care Of Business

I worked for the local newspaper during my senior year of high school and after high school I worked one job after another, ranging from loading trucks for Pepsi Cola, to security. The security job was kind of nice as I was the relief man for all those who worked five days a week. I worked two days at Whirlpool, two days at the local college, and one day at the hospital. When the position came up for the full-time position at the college, I took it, as I only lived about two blocks away and could walk to and from work.

The hardest part about this job was keeping the guys out of the girls' dorm so the girls felt safe. Each day at four o'clock in the morning the lady who baked for the college would show up for work. Because it was so dark in the alley where she had to park and enter the building I would always meet her there with the doors already unlocked and the lights turned on inside. She was like a grandmother to me and would make sure there were some cookies, or whatever treat she was concocting that day, set aside for me. It was around this time in the morning when I received a call that there had been a break-in in the girls' dorm. Well, the kitchen was also in the girls' dorm building so I went outside and began to scope out the building from the outside. As I rounded the building towards the front there was a young man dressed in dark clothing so I stopped him and asked him for his ID. He produced an ID and an excuse of why he just happened to be near the girls' dorm right at that particular moment. I was just a security guard and did not have authority to hold anyone and the police were not on the scene yet so I had to let him go. As it turned out he had gone into the girls' dorm and robbed one of the girls at knife point. I had caught him as he was leaving the building although I never saw him exit the building. Based on my description he was later apprehended and charged with the robbery.

During the Christmas season the school would close for two weeks and everyone would go home. Well, almost everyone that is, except the one girl who had been robbed just a month before. She did not get to go home. She saw me as I was doing my security checks on her building and came to the door and asked me to come into the building with her for a while. Now as a young man I did not mind a young lady taking notice of me but it made me nervous to be in that building all alone with her. I was there to protect her, but who was going to protect me if she wanted to make up a story about me. I wrote up in my report that I was uneasy guarding in a girls' dorm and from then

CHAPTER 4: TAKING CARE OF BUSINESS

on they added another female guard to be in the girls' dorm and I took care of the rest of the campus.

The main hall was the oldest building on campus and it was over one hundred forty years old when I was there. I always figured as I walked through these buildings that if I had a light on, and someone was in there, then they would know where I was and see me coming. However, if I walked through in the dark with only the light from the exit signs, then my eyes would adjust and they would not know where I was. Walking through the old main hall was nerve-racking because it was so old, it always sounded like there was someone walking behind you or on the next floor above you. After a while though, you would get used to the usual sounds and it wasn't so bad.

One night, as I was checking the athletic building (gym), I noticed that one of the doors was ajar. I opened it and looked into the gym, but saw nothing, so I started to close it when I heard another door in the gym open. I ran back inside just in time to see it close. It was the door leading to the men's' locker room, so I secured the outside door and made my way to the men's locker room. Now every door was already locked so you had to have a key to get through them, and as I opened the door to go into the men's locker room, I heard another door open and close. That door was the one that led from the locker room into the coach's office, so I opened it, and as I did I could hear yet another door open and shut. The next door went from the coach's office into an observatory under the surface level of the pool. So I kept on opening doors and I kept hearing other doors opening and closing just ahead of me, but I could never seem to catch up. This pursuit proceeded out through the women's locker room side and back out into the gym. As I ran out into the gym there was yet another outside door just swinging closed. I ran out through the door but there was no one in sight. This was no figment of my imagination; there was someone who had keys, and they kept just a few steps in front of me as I was trying to catch them. When I wrote this up in my report and my supervisor read it, he looked at me and said, "So what would you have done if you had caught them?" I had not thought about that. It could have been more than one person, and they may have been able to take me out of the picture. That never crossed my mind that night, but the next time I saw a door open, I just locked it and wrote it up in my log.

When I was still working at the hospital one night a week, I noticed a window ajar in one of the doctor's office buildings behind the hospital. Those buildings were part of our responsibility to check, so when I found this window open, I called the police. They arrived a few minutes later and I opened the building

CHAPTER 4: TAKING CARE OF BUSINESS

for them so we could all go in and check things out. The one officer went off on his own while I stayed with the other officer, at least within easy speaking distance. We went all through the building from office to office, as they were all interconnected, and did not find a thing. So we came back to the window and shut it and locked it. Then we stepped outside and locked the building back up. The two officers and I stood there talking for a little bit when all of a sudden there was a loud noise inside the building we had just searched. I unlocked the door and again we went in. This time they had their guns drawn and did a sweep from room to room. All of a sudden one shouted "I've got 'em." The burglar had been hiding in the false ceiling in one of the offices. When he thought we had left, he made his move to start getting back down and fell through the ceiling tiles, crashing onto the floor below. The good news was that they did not have to take him far to have him checked out for injuries as the hospital was just across the parking lot. Thus the excitement of a security guard. But, it was a living.

That summer while I was on vacation I stopped by my dad's for a visit. I had been under heavy conviction for over a year and could not take it any longer. I got up on Saturday morning and went into the living room where Dad was already up and reading his Bible. I looked him in the eye and said, "Dad, I can't run any longer. I can't take any more of this. I NEED to get SAVED!" Dad simply said, "Then I guess it is about time we prayed." That is when I finally found the peace and rest that I had wanted but was unwilling to accept. I knelt right there in my father's living room and confessed my sins before God the Father, asking him to forgive me and save my wretched soul. Do you know what happened next? HE DID! He saved me right then and there! AMEN! August second, nineteen eighty on Saturday morning Jesus Christ saved this poor old wretched sinner and I became a child of God! AMEN! Just writing it down and thinking about it all makes me want to shout and Praise His Holy Name! AMEN!

> I left for vacation Lost,
>
> I returned from vacation Found,
>
> I left a God forsaken sinner,
>
> I returned a God-Redeemed Sinner,
>
> I left a miserable child of my father the devil,
>
> I returned a Glorious Child of my Father, JEHOVAH my precious Lord and Saviour, God the Father, God the Son and God the Holy Spirit!
>
> PRAISE GOD HE SAVED MY SOUL!!!

If that doesn't give you something to shout about you'd better get your SHOUTER checked!

CHAPTER 4: TAKING CARE OF BUSINESS

After all I had been through I had to take one last thought. I decided to accept Jesus Christ as my Lord and Saviour. Will you do the same? Turn to page 178, right now. Go ahead, turn there and read the Gospel Tract called:

"One Last Thought"

You can always come back to this page later on. **Go on then... get it settled with God!!!**

After getting saved I decided to move closer to my dad, but I did not immediately rush out and join a church. After my parents divorced, the time we spent with our father (although I believe he was saved) led to much confusion in my life and only added to why it took so long for me to get saved in the first place. Whether it was during the weekends that we spent with him or the six weeks every summer, it seemed like every time we visited, he was in another church. We were taken to so many it would be difficult to list them all, and probably be some of the most boring reading, so I'll not list them all. Let me just say that we had been taken to all of the major denominations and most of the other ones that few know about. On top of these there were the "fellowships" that were not really churches at all but just a bunch of people who were disenchanted (upset) with organized religion.

All of these different religions had their beliefs on which bible was a good one, and their own interpretation of what that book meant to them. The problem is that once you begin visiting all these religions you will notice that none of them agree with each other. No wonder so many people get discouraged and leave church disillusioned. Yet when they leave and start their own little group, it becomes just another religion following this same pattern. I am so tempted here to begin preaching that I must exercise

CHAPTER 4: TAKING CARE OF BUSINESS

some self-control as I will deal with the "preachy" part later on. Anyway, because of all these different religions that I had been exposed to, and the fact that they all thought they were right but none of them agreed with each other, left a huge question in my mind as to which church is the TRUE church. Ok, just a little preaching. Jesus said in the Scriptures: *And I say also unto thee, That thou art Peter, and upon this rock I will build my church; and the gates of hell shall not prevail against it. Matthew 16:18* This verse has been taken out of context by many religions to say that Jesus appointed a spiritual leader here on earth starting with Peter, but that is not the meaning of this verse. The word Peter means pebble, but Jesus, in this passage, said he would build His Church upon "this ROCK" and was referring to himself.

Matthew 21:42 *"Jesus saith unto them, Did ye never read in the scriptures, The stone which the builders rejected, the same is become the head of the corner: this is the Lord's doing, and it is marvellous in our eyes?"* He was quoting from *Psalms 118:22-23 The stone which the builders refused is become the head stone of the corner. 23 This is the LORD'S doing; it is marvellous in our eyes.*

Back to the point. If Jesus said He would build His Church and the gates of Hell would not prevail against it, then His Church had to be out there somewhere.

Perhaps one of these "religions" I had been exposed too was right, but which one? This is why I did not rush out to join a church but instead started reading my Bible, studying, looking for the "Marks of a New Testament Church." I then took these "Marks" and started revisiting all those denominations I had been raised in. One by one they failed to match the New Testament Church as I had found in Scripture. I began to question if I had taken the correct approach to finding a church or not when I visited a Southern Baptist Church. It did not match completely, but it was definitely a whole lot closer than anything I had been to thus far.

Within a year of being saved and joining a church I began to sense that God was calling me into the ministry, wanting something more for my life. With all the confusion I still had from the influences of so many religions, I did not know what to do, so I just kept it to myself and went on with life. See page 190 for the Gospel Tract "Confusion."

When I moved up north near my dad, I got a job working in a small print shop in an area that had over thirty percent unemployment and I was told I could not find work up there. I also worked with my dad who had his own business doing interior and exterior decorating. That is a fancy way of saying that we did wall-papering and painting, and some light

CHAPTER 4: TAKING CARE OF BUSINESS

construction. After about a year I quit the printing job and just worked with Dad as business had picked up enough to support the both of us.

During the summer we would work mostly outside projects and during the winters we would focus on the inside jobs that came along. Most of the equipment that my dad owned, he had owned for a long, long time. There were countless times that this equipment, although well maintained, simply failed. Some of these failures are kind of funny (NOW) but at the time they were, well, stressful to say the least.

One I remember well was when we were painting the outside of a house and I was trimming out a window that was on the second floor of the house. I was at least twenty-four feet in the air on a wooden ladder that had aluminum feet on the bottom of it. When trimming a window that far up in the air we would often shift the top part of the ladder from side to side of the window to get the best angles for trimming. It was during one of these shifts from side to side that one of those aluminum feet collapsed and folded in half, causing the ladder to begin sliding down the side of the house. I quickly dropped my brush, put my feet on the outside of the ladder and did what is called a "fireman's slide" down the ladder. At the bottom you would just simply tuck and roll when hitting the ground. This procedure allowed you to get down quickly with as few injuries as possible. Other than bruised pride, the only injury was to the ladder, so I had to do surgery and remove both the aluminum feet. After that happened it took me nearly twenty years to again trust any ladder made out of aluminum.

There was another time that Dad and I were putting up soffit on a single-story house using a ladder that was over twenty years old. (*Keep your safety comments to yourself.*) Anyway... it was an extension ladder that we separated into two pieces and used ladder jacks to put scaffolding across between the two ladders. This gave us access to much of the eave under the edge of the house at one time without having to move the ladder much. Well, as long as we stayed at separate ends of the scaffold it was fine, BUT... Yeah, eventually we both ended up on the same end and SNAP, CRACKLE, POP, and I am not talking about the cereal. The ladder on Dad's end broke and we both fell towards the ground. I was the lucky one as I hit the ground and as I said before, I just tucked and rolled away from the crashing equipment. Dad, on the other hand, did not get away so lucky. He had the privilege of "riding the rail" as the scaffolding turned sideways and Dad landed with one leg on either side of it as it fell with a sudden stop as it hit the ground.

The worst thing that ever happened was when we were hired to wallpaper a living room for an elderly

CHAPTER 4: TAKING CARE OF BUSINESS

woman. In order to do the job right we had to remove the layers and layers of wallpaper that were already on the walls. If I remember correctly there were at least eight layers and you could see where the seams were overlapped leaving bumps everywhere in the paper. Dad had a wallpaper steamer for heating up the wallpaper so the glue would release and you could easily pull the old paper off of the walls. After removing all the furniture, setting up our equipment, including fans in the windows to draw in fresh air, and covering the floor, we started steaming the walls and pealing the paper off. Dad was standing up operating the steamer and I was bending over scraping the small remaining pieces off the wall. As we worked I began to get a headache and mentioned this to Dad several times. He just thought that because I was working with my head down that it was interfering with the flow of blood, causing the headache.

We continued to work as my headache continued to get worse and worse. We were making good progress and did not want to stop; just to get it over with. By now Dad also had a headache and was slowing down, but he was in his late sixties so I thought very little about it. The next thing I knew I heard a THUMP and looked to see Dad slumped against the wall slowly sliding down to the ground and passing out. I dropped my scraper, grabbing Dad and dragging him out of the room which we had sealed off from the rest of the house. Once I got Dad out of the room, I went back into the room and turned off the steamer and tried to crawl out of the room. I know I passed out in the room and do not have any clue as to how long I was in there before regaining consciousness and crawling the rest of the way out of the room. Dad was still lying there on the floor and I asked him several times if he was all right, with no response, and then I passed out again.

The lady who owned the house was not home, and, in fact, had made arrangements to stay with her daughter while we were working in her home. As near as we could figure, we laid there on the kitchen floor between three to four hours before regaining consciousness. Even after regaining consciousness, we still laid there in agonizing pain for at least another hour or so. Once Dad was physically able to move again I took him home and called another friend of ours to come help me finish the job the next day. We put two more fans in the windows and picked up where Dad and I left off the day before. I still had a headache but we needed to get the job done, so I had to put up with it. It took nearly four hours to completely strip all the paper off the walls and ceiling of that room but at least it was done. The man who helped me finish the job, after going home, decided to go to the hospital to get checked out because the headache he had was so

CHAPTER 4: TAKING CARE OF BUSINESS

bad. I went home and crashed for two days, mostly sleeping as it seemed that nothing would relieve the headache.

The man who went to the hospital found out that we had gotten formaldehyde poisoning and after a treatment of pure oxygen his headache diminished considerably. From that time on when we would call him to help us he would say "I'm not stripping wallpaper again!" As it turned out, the wallpaper on the top was the kind that you needed to use a wall steamer to remove, but the next two layers contained formaldehyde in the paste, which allowed this type of wallpaper to be easily strippable. When we used the steamer to heat up the top layer we knew that we would also heat up all the other layers, but we did not know about the formaldehyde. This is a rough way to learn a lesson, but learn we did, and refused any job that required removing wallpaper after that. We would tell the homeowners how to do it, where to rent the equipment, and warn them about formaldehyde poisoning.

I have one more story to tell about my dad, at least for this chapter. When I was a young boy and trusted my dad without question, I went on a job with him where he was patching some holes in the drywall to prep it for painting. He had just opened a new can of "DAP," which was quick drying putty for patching small holes. When you opened a new can there was always a small amount that stuck to the lid and Dad asked me if I had ever smelled it, as he offered the lid, holding it towards my nose. TRUSTING my dad I leaned toward the outreached hand of my dad and took a deep sniff just as he thrust the lid up toward me and shoved my nose full of "DAP" putty. So much for trusting Dad, especially when he had that little grin on his face.

Years later we were painting the outside of a cottage on the lake. I was working on the ladder up in the peak and Dad was on the scaffold down below. In our family most of the men, including my dad, have a hereditary bald spot on the top of our head. As I was painting the gable end of this house with Dad below, I noticed that bald spot moving back and forth underneath me and remembered that putty from my childhood. So the next time Dad passed under me I dripped a small glob of paint and hit a bull's-eye on his bald spot. Dad shouted, "HEY" and I said, "Oh, I'm sorry." A few minutes later there he was again, and yep, you guessed it. I dripped another small glob and hit a bull's-eye once again. Again Dad shouted, "HEY" and I said, "Oh I'm sorry." But I was not done, as Dad was standing right below me one more time. Yeah I sure did! I hit him one more time just for good measure. This time Dad looked up at me and said,

CHAPTER 4: TAKING CARE OF BUSINESS

"Hey, what are you doing?" to which I responded, "Do you remember the putty you pushed up my nose?" Dad laughed and said, "Yeah, but what has this got to do with that?" to which I exclaimed, "I have been patient and it is payback time." Dad reminded me that this paint was bought by the customer and I should not be wasting it on folly. He was right, but I still told him, "I'll buy them five gallons of paint" and let go of another big glob of paint "bull's-eye." Dad wasn't too happy with me that day, but the house got painted, as well as his bald spot, and we did not run out of paint. Oh yeah, and I felt better too!

> Ecclesiastes 3:1-8 *"To everything there is a season, and a time to every purpose under the heaven: A time to be born, and a time to die; a time to plant, and a time to pluck up that which is planted; A time to kill, and a time to heal; a time to break down, and a time to build up; A time to weep, and a time to laugh; a time to mourn, and a time to dance; A time to cast away stones, and a time to gather stones together; a time to embrace, and a time to refrain from embracing; A time to get, and a time to lose; a time to keep, and a time to cast away; A time to rend, and a time to sew; a time to keep silence, and a time to speak; A time to*

love, and a time to hate; a time of war, and a time of peace."

CHAPTER FIVE

You're In The Army Now

Right out of high school I wanted to serve in the military, and because two of my brothers had both been in the Air Force, I made that my first choice. I went to see a recruiter and he put me through all the tests and helped me determine what field of service I would like to be in. The scores from my ASVAB test were so good that I was told I could have any job I wanted and was offered a position as flight navigator. But I wanted to be a fighter pilot. The recruiter told me that there was a height requirement for fighter pilots and that I was too tall to fit in the cockpit. Still I felt that serving as a navigator would put me in a big slow bird, and that did not sound cool to me. (I was not thinking about the career I could have had after the military). The next position they offered me was MP, and since becoming a police officer was something I was interested in, I said, "Ok," and signed the papers. I was then taken to a large room and sworn into the United States Air Force delayed entry program. This meant I could finish high school and then right after graduation I would leave for basic training. The MP school I needed was not available until August so my entry date was the first week of July. When I reported for duty on my assigned date, I was weighed, and the recruiter said I was four pounds overweight and could not go. I argued with him for a short time that I would lose that weight in basic training, but he would not put me through. He sent me home for a month and said if I lost the weight he would then put me through. One month later when I weighed in I had gained another four pounds. The recruiter then told me I had the option of trying for one more month or I could be discharged and let that be that. I choose the second option as I was discouraged at this point and a few weeks later received an honorable discharge from the United States Air Force.

Four years later I got the bug again to serve in the military and went through the same processes. This time, like before, I did really well on the ASVAB test and was told I could have any job I wanted including duty on a nuclear sub. The thought of being in an enclosed tube submerged under water just did not set too well with me, so I was offered the position of Fire Direction. I thought this was some type of "fire fighter" or something like that. Boy, was I wrong. Fire Direction is part of the huge artillery cannons that are on a battleship. In the Fire Direction you get information from an observer of a target and you compute that data into firing data to send to the cannons so they can load up and hit the intended target. After spending the weekend in Detroit signing all the

CHAPTER 5: YOU'RE IN THE ARMY NOW

papers and getting sworn into the United States Navy, I was sent home until my entry day three days later.

About six hours after getting home from Detroit I received a phone call from my recruiter and he was very upset. I asked him what the problem was and all he would tell me was that I had to be in Detroit by 0800 in the morning. My dad took me to the bus station about forty miles from home so I could make it back to Detroit first thing in the morning. I traveled all night on the bus and arrived two hours before I needed to be there. I went into the "MEPPS" office and told them who I was and they took me immediately to another room, left me alone, and shut the door. I sat there for what seemed like forever and finally two men, one an officer and one an enlisted, entered. Both had been in the Navy for quite some time and of a high rank. The enlisted man began to question me about many subjects and continued this questioning for almost an hour. At the end of that hour, another two men came into the room and again the questioning began. This time it was more intense. They seemed angry about something, but would not tell me what I had done or what they were mad about. Again the questioning lasted for nearly an hour and they left the room. This went on all day, for over eight hours, during which time I was never given the opportunity for a glass of water or lunch. Finally after asking repeatedly for water, they gave me a glass. With each questioning session the person doing the questioning seemed more and more upset and aggressive towards me. I had no idea what was going on and no one would answer me when I asked for an explanation. With each passing hour of interrogation I was beginning to feel more like a caged animal than a human being.

Finally, when I had just about given up hope of ever seeing daylight again, I was taken upstairs to the "old man's" office (who just happened to be a woman). She was the senior ranking officer in charge of the MEPPS station and the first one who told me what was going on. I was being charged with fraudulent enlistment because what I had told the Air Force did not agree with what I had told the Navy. You see, I had told the Air Force that at the age of thirteen I had sleepwalked. It had been so long ago in my past that I had forgotten all about it and told the Navy that I had not sleepwalked past the age of thirteen. These are the questions that immediately jumped into my head. Sleep walking is a crime? THIS IS WHAT IT WAS ALL ABOUT?

The commander then, for the first time that day, asked me what I had to say in defense of these charges and for my side of the story. I sat there in her office and explained that what I had told the Air Force was true, but I had forgotten about it because it had been

CHAPTER 5: YOU'RE IN THE ARMY NOW

over nine years since it had happened and over four years since I had spoken or even thought about it. It was a simple case of forgetting and that was all there was to it. I told the commander that if forgetting was a crime (as I stretched out my arms in front of her and said), "Here they are. Lock me up and take me away." She then sent me out to her junior officer clerk and called him into her office. Soon he came back out and began typing a document, which, when he finished, and laid it in front of me, he told me to sign. I started to read it, as he reprimanded me to just sign the paper. I looked at him and told him that if it was all right, I'd read it first. The main part of the letter said these exact words, and I quote "I Russell Kidman upon my enlistment into the United States Navy did falsify information and have signed here in admission of this crime." I don't know about you but I slammed the paper back down in front of the clerk and said "NO WAY! I'll not sign this paper!" The clerk then took the paper back into the commander's office and soon appeared once again. This time he added another short paragraph to the above note which read something like this: Russell Kidman denies the above statement and has initialed here to confirm his denial.

That was reasonable enough for me so I initialed it where he instructed me too and was escorted down the stairs and out the door with the warning that I should never try to join the Navy again or these charges would once again be brought up against me. Then the warning was given that I should never try to join any military branch in the future either. They handed me a bus ticket for home and shoved me out the door. I told the commander that I knew of several guys who were doing drugs the night before and the Navy still took them, but because I had forgotten something, I was treated like an enemy of the state. You cannot begin to imagine how mad and thoroughly disgusted I was as I left there that day. On top of all that, how I had been so humiliated because I had forgotten something in my past was absurd. All I ever wanted to do was serve my country and at that point I felt like all I was to my country was trash. I went back home and enrolled in college while working as a courier driver for a bank, but the desire was not dead.

It took another three years for me to get the bug again, and get it I did. I was about to get my associate degree in drafting when I ran out of money for school. I was not aware of the fact that my drafting instructor had lined up a job in a local company for me as one of his two top students. He was planning on telling both of us after the end of the semester on Monday. Initially I was interested in the college money that was being offered through the Army Reserves, but when I went in to talk with the recruiter he showed me that being

CHAPTER 5: YOU'RE IN THE ARMY NOW

in the Active Army would benefit me more for college. Now consider the fact that I still had bitterness and hatred towards my step-dad. There was another man who I had thought was my friend until he tried to kill me. Let's just say I had some real strong anger issues and learning how to kill sounded pretty good to me.

In May of nineteen eighty-six, I enlisted in the United States Army and left for basic training. I had told the recruiter all about my previous two attempts at enlisting and his only question was, "Did you forget to tell me anything?" I laughed and said I'm smarter than that now. You see all legal documents from the U.S. government have the statement on them that says something to this effect: "I swear/ascertain that all statements herein contained are true to the best of my recollection and knowledge." I pointed to that statement on the enlistment forms and said, "This is my defense," to which we both just sat there and laughed.

Now it is important to understand my emotional condition when I enlisted in the Army and that I was backslidden from God, angry, and full of hatred. I had been misused by people who called themselves "Christians" and one of them was even a deacon in the church I had joined after getting saved. The issues with my mother had not been resolved at this point in time, and I was still mad at her for not believing us when we told her that her husband was abusing us and then leaving me on my own. To wrap it up in a nutshell, I was angry with the whole world!

The first day I arrived at basic training, I walked into the barracks and there was only one other person there, whose full name I often tell, but for the purpose of this book we will just call him Brian. Brian walked up to me and stuck out his hand to shake mine, so I returned the gesture as he said, and I quote: "I'm praying for you brother." NOW, I ask you, how did he know I was a "Brother"? Because I sure was not living like I was saved, but we had just met and how could he have known anything about me one way or the other? Every night he would come by my bunk and ask me if he could read the Bible with me. I would muster all the anger and resentment that I had towards "Christians" right then and just sneer at him telling him to "bug off" (not usually that nicely). The next night he would come back by and ask the same question again, and again I would cuss him up one side and down the other. This continued each night and each night I would get meaner and meaner towards him. I threatened to beat him up, and that did not stop him. I even threatened to kill him if he did not stop, and that didn't seem to faze him at all.

One Sunday we were ordered that, on this particular Sunday, we would all be going to church. I

CHAPTER 5: YOU'RE IN THE ARMY NOW

later found out that "my friend Brian" was responsible for this stunt. Anyway we "HAD" to go to chapel, so I obeyed orders and we were all marched down to the local chapel. The chaplain came out and he was a highly decorated major with a Catholic background. The "message" that day was not from the Bible nor did he ever quote or reference any passage from the Bible. He began with the title of his homily, loudly in a command voice: **"DO YOU HAVE THE FIRE IN YOUR EYES TO BE AN AIRBORN RANGER?"** For the next twenty or thirty minutes we had to sit there as he recruited for the "United States Army Rangers." I cannot emphasize enough that his message had absolutely nothing to do with God or the Bible! However, the Holy Spirit was well at work! All those times that Brian had come by my bunk, I did not want him to know it, but God was using him and he was getting through. The message that day that everyone else heard was, as I said, just recruitment for the Rangers, but what I heard was the tender voice of a loving Father trying to reach his fallen son. As I sit here writing this down I am fighting back the tears just thinking about the lengths our Father goes to, to retrieve his backslidden sheep.

That is the day I got right with GOD!!! I believe that there is a difference between getting saved and being converted. I was saved and under heavy conviction when I was converted. Consider what Jesus said to Peter just before he denied him three times:

Luke 22:31-32 *"And the Lord said, Simon, Simon, behold, Satan hath desired to have you, that he may sift you as wheat: But I have prayed for thee, that thy faith fail not: and when thou art converted, strengthen thy brethren."*

That day my life was changed from what God could do for me, to what I could do for Him, and I have never looked back. Many weeks later, as Brian and I were talking while polishing our boots, Brian said that he had no idea why he had joined the Army. I looked at him and just started to smile as I kept polishing my boots. I waited, and soon he said it again, but this time I did more than just smile. I looked him in the eye and said, "I know why you're here," rather emphatically. He looked at me with somewhat of a curious grin on his face and asked me what I meant by that. I simply said, "Because God sent you to bring me back to Him." Brian and I kept in touch for several years after basic training until he and I had both married and had other responsibilities. Who knows which one of us dropped the ball, but I know that I have never forgotten the obedient servant of Jesus Christ named Brian who God used to reach me, a backslidden sinner. By the way Brian, if you ever read this book, would you mind

CHAPTER 5: YOU'RE IN THE ARMY NOW

dropping me a line? I'd like to hear from you again.

    During basic training we learned so much information that I doubt if any book could contain all of it that was shoved down our throats. We also learned things that would help us to survive in combat like self-defense, chemical warfare, and rappelling. I had been looking forward to getting the opportunity to learn how to rappel down a cliff with much excitement. First they took us to a forty-foot tower where we learned the basics of rappelling. After several times down the tower I was ready to try my hand on the cliff. To get to the cliff we had to climb up a crevasse (which I had experience at from my years of living in New Mexico) so although I was far from the first one to start up the crevasse, I was the second one to reach the top. I ran over to where the rappel-master (drill sergeant) was standing and started to hook-up to go over the cliff. The rappel-master thought I was taking too long to accomplish my riggings so he did the second part for me. When he did this it caused me to have a faulty hook up where the rope did not cross itself, which is how the brake works. Because the rope ended up running alongside itself, I had no brake and could not slow down or stop my descent once on the cliff. I did not have enough experience to recognize the problem that had just been created, so I went ahead and leaned back over the edge of the cliff and started my rappel.

I had seen this done on TV so many times and could not wait to just throw out and jump, descending down the cliff in long bounds like a pro. I shoved out with my feet as I threw the rope out away from my body and started to descend. As I came back towards the face of the cliff I tried to set my brake and get another good footing but I could not stop, or even slow down. My weight was carrying me down the rope, and without being able to brake, it was soon obvious that stopping was going to be difficult. Because I was still moving at quite a fast pace down the face, when my feet hit against the cliff, I began to tumble head-over-heels. The man on rappel next to me had been a medic for a fire department as well as an instructor for rappelling. He kept up with me as best he could to shout commands on what to do trying to prevent any further injuries and trying to help me get my feet back under me. The cliff was over two hundred and sixty feet high and we were only rappelling about one hundred and sixty feet of that distance, to a platform that had been built on the face of the cliff. As I continued to tumble and fall, pushing my brake hand as far behind my back as possible, and gripping the rope as tightly as I could, I still was not slowing down. The friction between the nylon rope and my leather gloves was getting so hot that I could not hold on much

CHAPTER 5: YOU'RE IN THE ARMY NOW

longer. When I got a chance to get my feet back under me, I reached up with my free hand and grabbed the rope above me while making one last attempt to grasp the rope in my brake hand and stop. Although we were told not to do this, I began to slow down and finally after falling over one hundred and forty feet, I came to a stop just fifteen feet from the platform. I slowly made it the rest of the way down to the platform with the help of the former paramedic and was relieved to be back on solid ground.

The pain to my hands was so intense and can only be described by saying that it was like taking a cast iron pan and putting a fire under it. Then when the pan gets red hot, you pick it up with both hands and know that if you drop it you are going to die. When I told the drill sergeant on the platform that my hands were on fire, he pulled the gloves off my hands as gently as he could, and immediately there were blisters the size of baseballs on the palms of both hands. He popped them both, and the Army medic bandaged my hands. Because we were on bivouac and not back at the barracks, I was treated by the medic twice a day as he changed the bandages and put salve on my wounds. Next we headed over to the rifle range, where I qualified as a sharp shooter with third degree burns on both hands. It might also be noted that the qualifying took place in the rain as I had to lie in a puddle of water and mud with my burnt hands.

Finally, when we got back to the barracks, I was allowed to go to the clinic to have my hands looked at. I was sent to see a surgeon who scrapped the dead skin and tissue from my charred hands. He told me to let him know when he hit live nerves as I sat there and watched him cutting on my hands. All of a sudden he hit live tissue and I said, "Do.......c" and I passed out! The surgeon and his assistant went through six boxes of smelling salts to keep me alert so he knew when he was hitting live tissue.

My right hand was injured the worst, so it was wrapped each day with a special cloth that had been treated with chemicals to induce cell growth. As my hands began to heal, the skin between my thumb and first finger grew shorter and shorter until there was hardly any distance between them. When the surgeon noticed this was happening, he gave me an exercise to do by pushing my left thumb against my right thumb and the first fingers of each hand against each other at the same time. This forced the healing area to stretch out and allowed proper healing to take place.

My left hand started to heal but suffered a little setback when my wounds were busted back open during hand-to-hand combat training. This training took place in an area that was predominately sand.

CHAPTER 5: YOU'RE IN THE ARMY NOW

With the wounds busted open and us fighting, ducking and rolling, it was inevitable that sooner or later sand would get into the wounds. With all wounds healing, and graduation from basic training just around the corner, we had our last "dress uniform" inspection, with the sergeant major doing the inspecting. While I was getting ready, the former paramedic who had helped me during the repelling accident came over and was looking over my uniform when he noticed that my left hand was all puffed up. He turned my arm over and there was a deep red line running from the palm of my hand up past my elbow. He looked me in the eye and said, "I don't want to scare you, but if this is not looked at, it will kill you." He called the drill sergeant over to look at my hand and for the first time he treated me like a human instead of a recruit. He asked if I would stand in the inspection and as soon as it was over he would send me to the hospital.

After the inspection I went back to the barracks and changed my uniform and reported to the first sergeant's office. As I walked in, the first sergeant looked at me and with a self-righteous attitude said, "And what is wrong with you now?" I did not say a word. I just showed him my arm with the blood poisoning and, just like the drill sergeant, his attitude changed. He quickly drove me to the hospital himself. Yes I had blood poisoning from my left hand burns getting infected when we were training in the sand pit. I was put on antibiotics and within a few weeks all the infection was gone and my hands were starting to heal.

Even after basic training was over, I had to continue to go to the hospital for treatments to my hands and therapy to get the use of them back again. I lost one tendon that goes between your thumb and first finger on my right hand, but other than that they healed fine. Because the treatments to my hands continued during my "advanced training" I missed a couple of classes that were mandatory for my job and I had to have them to graduate. I ended up taking those classes at the end of my training cycle with another unit. I was awarded my first Army achievement medal for graduating from my advanced training, with not only the highest score in my class, but the best score that had ever been recorded for that military occupation. To back this up, and I will talk more about it later, not only was I book smart, but I became one of the best at my job in the entire U.S. Army.

CHAPTER SIX

An Help Meet For Him

Genesis 2:18 *"And the LORD God said, It is not good that the man should be alone; I will make him an help meet for him."*

After spending the entire summer in training in the heat of Oklahoma and graduating from both Army Basic Training and Advanced Individual Training, I was given leave for eleven days. I hopped on a flight back to Michigan, picked up my car, and started visiting friends and family who had not seen me for over five months. You see during Basic and "AIT" I had lost over fifty pounds and was now a lean, mean, fighting machine, wanting to show off to my friends.

There was one person in particular whom I had kept in contact with all during my training. I couldn't wait to get back to Michigan to visit her, but maybe I should put this in a different light first. We had several classes together in college and although I was interested in getting to a point that we would one day "date," I was content to be "just friends" for the time. There were many phone calls and letters exchanged while I was in training and it seemed that we were moving more toward that type of a relationship, so you

ALLOWED TO LIVE

can understand why there was some excitement and anticipation of seeing this person again. When I got back to Michigan I called her several times and left messages that I would be there and gave her the days and times I would be able to visit but never reached her on the phone. When I arrived in my old "college town" I called again, but there was no answer. Let's just say that I only had a few days to spend in the area before going to see my parents and during that time I called three times a day but she was not answering the phone. I drove out to her house and sat there waiting for hours, twice, but no one was home. There were some others that I wanted to see and so I made those arrangements and had dinner with another lady that evening. I wanted to look sharp so I wore my Army dress uniform and we had an enjoyable dinner. When I asked her if she wanted to go out dancing for the evening she declined and we went our separate ways.

Before going into the Army I was not living for God and, let's just face it, I was still not living a separated life (lack of teaching and another story). That night I went back to the club where I had hung out with friends before, but this time it was not to drink, but just to see my friends and let them see the change that had taken place in my life. Now once again I must add that after getting right with God during basic training I had started praying, asking God

CHAPTER 6: AN HELP MEET FOR HIM

to provide me with the woman he wanted me to be with for the rest of my life. I had given God a "short list" of sorts of what I thought would be nice in a wife, like that her heart would be sold out for God, facial features, height, and hair and eye color. Go ahead, you can laugh or make fun all you want, but I believe that God, although he knows our hearts, still wants us to ask for those things which mean the most to us. So that is how I prayed.

As I walked into the club that night I noticed that the eyes of most of the women in the place were following me as I walked about. Several of these women even stopped me and spoke to me which was something I was not used to, but attributed this to the fact that I was in uniform and the old saying "women like men in uniform." When I looked at the booth where my friends and I would usually sit, I noticed that there were five extremely pretty girls sitting in that particular booth. Because I was always drawn to pretty faces, I had asked God that when I met the girl he wanted me to be with, He would have her ask me out. That way I would know she was the one. Understand that at this time it was not an acceptable practice for the girl to ask the guy out on a date, but that is what I asked for. The more I walked around the room looking for my friends (none of which were there that night) I kept looking at those five girls in "my booth" and finally put it in my head that I was going to have to be leaving the next day so I might as well have as much fun as I could that night. At that point I walked up to the girls and introduced myself. To my surprise one of the young ladies spoke up and began introducing the rest of the group. She named them one by one as I would lean over the table and shake their hand and then she got to the last one and after introducing her to me she ended her little speech with, and I quote, "Don't you two make a cute couple?" We just looked at each other and laughed at the thought as I found myself a seat with all of them. Then the waitress came by and took our drink orders as each of the girls ordered a mixed drink except for one, yeah, the last one I was introduced to, she ordered a diet coke. Needless to say that when I ordered a regular coke myself and excused myself away from them for a moment they all looked at the last girl and said, "This one's yours 'cause he's not drinking!"

When I came back into the room, I asked if any of them wanted to dance and they all suggested that the last one, "Cathy," and I go dance. So we did. There was something different about her and it intrigued me to the point that I wanted to spend some time just talking with her. So, for the next two hours we went out into the lobby of the building, sat down on a couch, and just talked, getting better acquainted with one

CHAPTER 6: AN HELP MEET FOR HIM

another. Most of what either of us remembers from that night was how we would stare into each other's eyes like we were looking into a looking glass of the soul. She told me how she had not wanted to go out that night because she knew her friends would all be drinking, but she didn't want to be alone in the room either, and that was why she was there. Throughout the rest of that evening we danced and talked, and then she finally looked at me and asked if I would take her out for her birthday, which was in two days. I asked her where she lived, and when she told me, I knew I was not going to be anywhere close during my travels, so I said no. After another hour or so, once again she looked at me and asked, "Are you sure you cannot take me out for my birthday?" to which I replied, "Well, I'll think about it" and left it at that. Soon it was time to leave for the evening and I asked if I could drive her back to her hotel where they were staying. As it turns out, they were all hair dressers who had come to a cosmetology convention. One of the other girls, who I found out was this young lady's boss, pointed her finger at me and said, "You'd better bring her right behind us and if you touch her, I'll kill you." Somehow I believed her too!!! When we got to her room the other girls went inside as we stood outside and talked some more. Finally, she looked me in the eye and asked one more time if I would take her out for her birthday in two days. Persistence paid off as this time

I said yes. However, it meant I would not get to see my dad as long as I had planned, but now I had said yes, so I kissed her goodnight and she went into her room. As I drove away from where she was staying and headed back to my friend's house where I was staying, it hit me that she had asked me out and I almost blew it.

Guess where I was two days later? Yup, you're right. I drove down to take her out for her birthday and what a night that turned out to be. My car was loaded down with things I was taking with me, so for that night we took her car. She allowed me to drive so I helped her into the passenger side and then got in and started the car. When the car started, the radio came on, and it was tuned to a Christian radio station. I can honestly say at that moment I knew without any doubt that she was the one. Her parents allowed me to stay with them for the next four days as we spent more time together meeting her family and learning more about each other too. Her aunt just happened to stop by that first night I was there and as she came through the door, looked right at me and asked when we were getting married. We looked at each other kind of in shock after that, but as we have talked throughout our many years together, we both knew that night that God was in this and our prayers were being answered.

CHAPTER 6: AN HELP MEET FOR HIM

Well, my leave time was up and I had to head down to Fort Hood, Texas to my first duty station, so we said our goodbyes and I left. When I had a couple of days to ponder all that had happened during those short days I took some time to pray about the matter and God assured me that she was the one. I went to the PX (Post Exchange store) and bought a very nice card and in it I asked her to marry me and dropped it in the mail. I was sharing this story with a buddy of mine that I had just met and he stopped me in my tracks when I told him about the card and he said, "You cannot propose in a card!" He handed me a couple of dollars and then said, "Go call her and do it right now, man." So I did, and when I asked her to marry me over the phone there was no hesitation, just a very simple yet excited YES!!!

Later I learned that she stood there crying her eyes out as I had driven away from her parent's house that day, but her dad came up and put his arm around her and said, "Don't worry honey, he'll be back." When she got off the phone that day her mother asked her, "Did he just ask you to marry him?" and she said, "YES." Then her mother said, "And what did you say?" and she replied, "YES." We started planning a mid-summer wedding but ended up moving it up to December as that was the only time I could get leave to come back home and get married. That young lady became my wife on December 27, 1986 and we have been happily married ever since. At the publishing of this book we have been married now for twenty-seven years and people who meet us, as well as those who have known us for some time, tell us we act like newlyweds too much of the time. While we were taking a walk several years ago, holding hands and looking at each other, more than where we were going, there was another couple who approached us from the opposite direction and asked us how long we had been married, to which I replied, "We are newlyweds; we've only been married for twenty-five years now." The other couple stopped and looked at us in shock because of that answer, and were amazed at how close we still were. The Scripture comes to mind:

> Ecclesiastes 3:14 *"I know that, whatsoever God doeth, it shall be for ever: nothing can be put to it, nor any thing taken from it: and God doeth it, that men should fear before him."*

Other than my salvation, this is the greatest thing that has ever happened to me. God not only gave me His salvation, but also His choice for my bride. Here is a thought for you, the reader: Why is it that we can trust God with the Eternality of our soul but refuse to trust Him for His choice of a mate for our live? WE HAVE NO REGRETS!!!

CHAPTER SEVEN

Battle Ready, Sir

My first duty station was at Fort Hood, Texas with the First Battalion Third Field Artillery, a unit that was well decorated in World War II, Korea, and Vietnam. There was a popular TV program on back then called "The A-Team" and as I walked up the stairs to the third floor where our Battery Headquarters were located, I noticed that on the door was this same label "A-Team." On the TV show the "A-Team" could do anything, and it made me feel, as well as understand, that I was part of something bigger than myself.

My rank was PFC which stands for Private First Class which also means I was low on the pecking order and had to work my way up the ladder of rank and respect. My combat duties were as part of the advance party (one person from each cannon and fire direction sections who would travel ahead of the regular unit to prepare our fighting positions for the regular unit to arrive and be ready to fire as soon as they pulled in), along with my duties as the advance party person for Alpha first platoon FDC, I was also the driver for the gunnery sergeant who was in charge of the advance party.

Although separated by four pay grades in rank,

Gunny and I became good friends and would discuss matters of military duty, politics and religion. Gunny was a Seventh-day Adventist and I was a Baptist so you can imagine what some of our conversations were like. Even with all the differences in what we believed we still remained friends throughout our time together. One of the last conversations we had got very deep and intense to say the least. After much debate for several hours I looked at Gunny and said, "Gunny, if you really believed what you say you believe, you would live it." It was quiet inside that hummer for a long time and then he replied... "You're right, I should." What he said next is what encouraged me the most though; he said, "That is what bothers me, because you do." He then commented on how I did live what I "preach" and how that made an impression on him. I have not seen him since then but one never knows what seeds were planted.

Anyway I have a few stories to tell about some of our adventures during our times together in our hummer. Many times our "advance party" duties took place at night and on this one particular night we were leading a deuce and a half truck full of the other team members to our next location when we noticed that they were not behind us any longer. Gunny told me to stop, so there we were sitting in the middle of the road with no lights on, waiting for the deuce to catch up to

CHAPTER 7: BATTLE READY, SIR

us, when I noticed it coming over the little hill behind us. The deuce was moving, and I mean moving, to say the least. I had just seconds to make a decision of what to do in order to avoid the deuce running into the back of our hummer. I floored the hummer, steering it through a deep ditch, and almost tossing Gunny out the door as we narrowly avoided being hit. While bouncing around in the hummer as we went through the ditch, Gunny looked at me and said "WHAT ARE YOU DOING?" Before I could answer, the deuce flew by us just narrowly missing the back of the hummer. When everything finally stopped bouncing around as the hummer came to a stop, Gunny just looked at me and said, "OH" because he had figured it out.

When traveling in a military convoy you are supposed to stay behind the vehicle right in front of you. The reason for this is because in combat the road traveled may be mined, so you follow the lead vehicle because their path is clearly safe. All that was said to tell the next story which happened while we were on a thirty-day training exercise at the National Training Center (NTC) in Fort Erwin, California. We were traveling through a simulated mine field; the battery commander was the lead vehicle, then Gunny and I in our hummer, followed by that same deuce and a half. The Captain proceeded down a steep hill and then told his driver to stop about two car lengths past the bottom of the hill. Being second in the lineup of vehicles, I drove our hummer down the steep grade, stopping right behind the captain's vehicle as it still just sat there just past the bottom of the hill. I looked in my rearview mirrors, and, low and behold, there was that stupid deuce creaming down the hill. Now let me say this while I keep you in suspense. There was not any more room at the bottom of the hill for another vehicle and I knew that the deuce was having braking problems. Ok, back to the deuce creaming down the hill. So again I punched the hummer, steering it off into the simulated mine field, as the deuce again flew past us, just narrowly missing us, and smashing into the captain's hummer, as the driver of the deuce did all he could to stop his truck. The captain was not hurt and there was very little damage to his hummer, but had we stayed where we had been, we would have been severely injured. Although I had broken protocol and in a real combat situation may have gotten us killed, as I saw it, we were probably dead either way.

It seems that most of my problems while stationed at Fort Hood involve a deuce and a half, and this third incident is no exception. Our tracked vehicle was in for repairs and some updates so we were operating out of a deuce. At one position where we were parked we were within a hundred feet or so of our second platoon

CHAPTER 7: BATTLE READY, SIR

counterpart (FDC) who was still operating out of their tracked vehicle. It was kind of cool for Texas weather and our deuce driver was trying to get some much needed rest. With all the equipment we had running in the back of the deuce, it was often left running to keep the electrical power supplied to that equipment. I was standing right behind our captain who was leaning into the open door on the back of our second platoon's tracked vehicle talking with the lieutenant in that vehicle. The driver of the deuce, as mentioned before, was asleep in the cab of the deuce when he accidently knocked the shifter into reverse and the deuce lunged backward, picking up speed as it raced toward where the captain and I were standing. The captain was unaware of the impending danger as I grabbed him, pulling him away from the tracked vehicle and wrestling him to the ground a safe distance away, just as the deuce creamed into the tracked vehicle. The captain was at first outraged that a private had handled him in such a rough manner, but when the deuce collided with the tracked vehicle just seconds later, he understood without further explanation that he would have been killed had I not grabbed him like I did. Although I received no military medals for what I had done in each of these incidents, lives were saved and I had earned the respect of those in leadership above me.

While at Fort Hood I also had a corporal who was,

in my opinion, one of the meanest people whom I had ever met in my life. He got under my skin so badly that I began to pray that God would get him out of my life. Just two weeks later he received orders sending him to Korea. I was so happy, and as a young Christian somewhat amazed that God had answered my prayer, let alone so quickly. However, my dear reader, one must be careful what they "pray" for. You see I had asked God to take him out of my life but I never considered that I needed to pray about who would be brought in.

One week later our new corporal showed up and he made the one that had just left look like a puppy. This new corporal would be a real thorn in my flesh for many months to come while we were both stationed together. He had one of the most vile mouths I had heard yet in my short military career, and the taking of God's name in vain was not a problem for him either. Every time he would use God's name in vain, I would reply with something like, "God's last name is not..." and he would get mad at me, making me do pushups or some dirty job that needed to be done.

One day as we were out in the field training, he began to curse again using God's name in vain, to which I gave my usual response. This time though he looked at me and said, "I order you not to talk about God in my presence any longer!" I looked at him and

CHAPTER 7: BATTLE READY, SIR

said, "That is an illegal order." I waited for a moment, and then said, "But I am willing to obey it if you will stop bringing up His name!" There was a long silent pause before the corporal looked me in the eye and said, "I can't do that," to which I replied, "Then neither can I." God honored that stand I took with this ungodly man and many months later, as I was leaving Fort Hood, this same corporal took me aside in his room and said with tears in his eyes, "Don't ever stop praying for me." I have not heard from him since that day but I have continued to pray for him throughout all these many years. God only knows whatever became of this man but I am assured that God used me to reach one who before was unreachable. Just a note that I have assurance because of what takes place a few years down the road, but for now I'll leave it at that.

The military has a way of not keeping you anywhere for very long before it's time to move or PCS; that means Permanent Change of Station, this time to Baumholder, Germany. Not only was I being sent to another duty station; I was being sent overseas to a foreign country. My wife was now "in the family way" with our first child and I was being told that she could not travel with me to Europe, but would have to travel on her own several months down the road. We asked our Christian friends to join us in prayer about this matter and then we left it up to the Lord. Just a couple of weeks before I was to leave Fort Hood my orders were changed and my wife (seven months along with child) was granted permission to travel with me to Germany. The U.S. Army provided us with first class tickets on a DC10 headed for Frankfurt, and away we went. That was the only time we have flown first class and will more than likely be the last too.

Did I mention that my wife was with child? Did I also mention that she gets motion sickness? Did I mention that she was traveling with me? Oh yeah, did I mention that she got sick on the flight and regurgitated her dinner all over my lap (I was in my class A Uniform)? Just because we were in first class does not mean that we had a leisurely, wonderful flight. Yeah, it doesn't mean that at all.

Once on the ground in Germany, I was so thankful, as I went into the restroom and washed up and cleaned my uniform as best as I could. Then came the bad news. We had a seven-hour bus ride to the base where I was stationed, and the bus stopped at what seemed like every little base there was between Frankfurt and Baumholder, following all the winding and twisting roads that only added to my wife's nausea and further perfuming of my uniform. To say the least, by the time we arrived in Baumholder, we both looked a real mess and I did not smell too impressive either. We were picked up by a staff sergeant and taken by car to

CHAPTER 7: BATTLE READY, SIR

Battalion Headquarters where I was to go in and meet the command sergeant major. As I got out of the car and put my hat on (tired and sleep deprived) I guess I put my cap on backwards and this staff sergeant began to chew me out, to which I responded, "Look sergeant, I've been up for over thirty-six hours, my wife has thrown up on me at least three times in the past twenty-four hours, I am tired, and don't really care what you or the sergeant major thinks about it." I had never spoken to someone of a higher rank like that before, but I really did not care at that point. The sergeant grabbed my cap, turned it around and gently placed it back on my head the correct way and said, "Well, at least don't make me look bad, ok? Welcome to Germany!

Once again I was placed in Alpha Battery (A-Team) in my new unit Second Battalion, Twenty-ninth Field Artillery. The unit slogan and subtitle to this chapter is "Battle Ready, Sir." I would spend the next three-and-a-half years of my life in this unit and eventually would deploy to combat under her banner. Although there were many jokes we often told each other, and especially the "newbies," about our unit, I am today proud to say that I served our nation in this distinguished unit. But, we will address more on that later.

When we knew that we would be moving to

ALLOWED TO LIVE

Germany we began to pray and ask God for a place to live and an automobile that we could afford once we would arrive in country. We were put up in the Hotel on post until we could find housing out on the German economy. I had gone to housing where they had cards on the houses and apartments that were available for rent by American soldiers stationed there. I was just a Specialist E-4 so my income was somewhat limited, to say the least.

We looked at several apartments and then I remembered seeing a card on a two-bedroom house for rent on the same street where we had just looked at a small efficiency apartment. We walked down the street and as we turned into the driveway, we were met by an elderly man who walked very slowly. He was eighty-seven years old and a veteran of World War II who had been forced to serve in the German Army after immigrating to Germany from Italy as a young man. He spoke no English and I spoke no German, but we had been assigned a soldier who spoke German to help us get settled and he was with us. The old man said he had been waiting for us, which took us by surprise as we had not originally planned on looking at this property. He took us through the two bedroom home which was a garage that had been converted into a house. It was just what we had prayed for and when he told us the price we were floored. You see we had

CHAPTER 7: BATTLE READY, SIR

been told it would cost us about three thousand dollars a month to rent a house on the economy, but this one was only going to cost us six hundred and fifty-six Deutsche Marks per month, which was about three hundred and twenty-five dollars a month.

We had to go back to the housing department to register for this property, so we did just that in much haste. When we arrived at the housing department I quickly started searching through the cards for that property again. The problem is that the card was not there any longer. Any soldier could pick out a property and reserve it while they went to look at it, and the card would be taken out of the file and placed in a special book. When I could not find card in the file the clerk then looked in that special book and it was not there either, so she asked her boss what they should do. They did not have a current contract on the property but with the card missing the clerk did not know just what to do. Her boss said that there was another soldier that had wanted to look at that property but because the card was not in that special book, it was not reserved, so she gave the go-ahead for us to rent it. Just as the clerk typed our names on the contract the other soldier came in the door waving the card and said, "I'll take this house on Schubenstrasse Six." The head of the housing department grabbed the card out of his hand and said, "You were not allowed to take this card out of this office and because of that this property has already been rented out to this soldier," and pointed at me. That staff sergeant was not very happy, but we were, and just as we had prayed for a two bedroom house, God supplied.

Within the next two weeks we had found a church to attend which was just a couple of blocks from our house. After church one Sunday, one of the members came up to me and asked if we had a car. I said no and he handed me the keys to an older BMW. He then said he wanted eight hundred dollars for it but we could pay him whenever we could afford to do so. What he did not know is that we had our income tax refund coming and it was for seven hundred ninety-nine dollars and seventy-four cents. That means the car, a BMW, only cost us twenty-six cents out of our pocket. Again God had provided what we needed, as we needed it, according to His riches.

Within just a couple of months of arriving in Germany, my wife gave birth to our first-born, our son. He was born in an American Army Base hospital, the same one that our troops are medivaced to from combat. He was born in an American hospital on what is effectually American soil, but because he was born in Germany he was given dual citizenship as both an American and a German. This would also apply to our daughter who was born two years later in a German

CHAPTER 7: BATTLE READY, SIR

hospital, but it only applied until they were eighteen and then it reverted to one or the other depending on which country they were living in at the time, which was the United States of America.

With all that being settled, it was time to be a soldier again and very quickly I found out that being stationed in Germany was different from being stationed in the United States. Everything was taken more seriously. This applied especially to any and all training for combat. On the other hand, I found that the training, although tougher, provided more detail in its instruction and made those who would apply this learning into some of the best soldiers in the world.

During the next three years there were many deployments for one or more months at a time to training areas where we would improve our skills. Several of us in our battalion became competitive in doing our jobs, constantly seeking to be the best. We would study often and train hard during our exercises, constantly pushing each other to excel to be the best, which resulted in us all achieving awards and commendations left and right. We had the highest test scores for our M.O.S. (Military Occupational Service) throughout the ranks of the entire U.S. Army. We began to get a reputation for being the best the Army had to offer, especially in Europe. This would be the catalyst of why we ended up being called to serve in combat during Desert Shield and Desert Storm.

A Psalm of David.

Psalm18:34 *"He teacheth my hands to war, so that a bow of steel is broken by mine arms."*

A Psalm of David.

Psalm144:1 *"Blessed be the LORD my strength, which teacheth my hands to war, and my fingers to fight:"*

CHAPTER EIGHT
Persian Gulf War

"C-130 rolling down the strip, airborne daddy gonna take a little trip." That is how one of our cadences started and also applies to this chapter of my life. If I had not had to extend nine months in order to have my wife travel with me to Germany, I would have already been discharged and out of the service, but that was not the case. It was August 2nd of 1990 and I was nearing the end of my contract with just six months left to go in the Army when it happened. The TV was on in the TV room at Battery Headquarters when I walked by the room and something caught my attention, so I walked into the room where the first sergeant (Top), executive officer (XO) and our captain stood, eyes glued to the TV. Iraq had just invaded Kuwait and they were showing live footage of the conflict as it happened. We all stood there for a while, watching, and then one of them, I don't remember who, but probably the captain said, "You know that is our secondary field of deployment, don't you?" You could have heard a pin drop inside that room but those words would come to be true.

In the military there are many ways to advance oneself and one of those ways is to work into a position that is above your pay-grade. I had done that and for nearly a year now I was working, at least one weekend a month, in what we will call "the vault" in an E-7 pay-grade as an E-5 sergeant. This position required me to have and maintain a top secret security clearance and to spend up to twenty-four hours at a time in the vault. I cannot go into detail of what was in the vault other than to say our unit received its orders from the Pentagon through that office. About a week later in August, after the invasion of Kuwait, I received a message that required me to call in my whole team, which had never happened before. When we were done, in our hands were our unit's orders to deploy to Saudi Arabia as part of the Persian Gulf build-up and defensive against Iraq and Saddam Hussein.

We followed our protocol and called in the battalion commander and sergeant major to brief them on their orders from the Pentagon. Other than the direct staff of the battalion, commander and sergeant major, there were only four of us who knew what those orders said or that we had even received them. We were sworn to secrecy on the matter and I know for myself that I did not tell a soul about it, not even my wife or family. Our command began to act peculiar though, and started offering thirty-day passes to everyone for over the Christmas holiday period. Now you must understand that being in a combat unit in a

CHAPTER 8: PERSIAN GULF WAR

foreign country you are required to maintain at least eighty-percent of your troops in-country at all times, so this did not make sense to most of the soldiers, but, hey, they were going to get to go home for a month over Christmas, so what did they care about regulations? This kept minds busy planning on their leave time while the wheels of deployment began to roll. On November 10, 1990, just after returning from a two-month deployment for training, our battalion commander announced to the rest of the soldiers that their leaves were cancelled and we would be deploying to Saudi Arabia within two months' time. We had less than thirty days to get our vehicles loaded onto ships and on their way to the port of Duran and only about another thirty days to get our lives in order to deploy.

You see as I started this chapter off, I mentioned that I had only six months left before I was supposed to get out of the Army and that was going to fall just one month after we deployed. The President of the United States then issued an order freezing all combat MOS's, which meant that I was again being involuntarily extended until the needs of the Army were met. My cousin had been deployed to Vietnam under a similar situation and his family was tossed out of quarters and left on the street with nowhere to go and no way to get there because according to "orders"

ALLOWED TO LIVE

he had been discharged, but in truth he was in Vietnam. I was not going to let that happen to me and my family so in mid-August, Sergeant Kidman, who had talked so much trash about getting out of the Army, all of a sudden re-enlisted for another three years. Many of those with whom I served never understood why I did that until the fateful day our C-130 took off from Ramstein Air force base in Germany headed to Saudi Arabia. I had made a game of it I guess you could say, and would constantly tell our first sergeant that we were not really going, but as the wheels of the big bird lifted off the tarmac with us inside in full battle dress Top (1st Sgt) leaned over and looked at me and shouted, "Hey Kidman, you still think we ain't going?" to which I replied, "Yeah we're going, but it's only a training exercise" and everyone had a great laugh. I guess God used that to help calm everyone's nerves for the eight hour flight, sitting in nothing but a web harness, with your comrades closer to you than you ever thought you would want them.

I guess here is as good a place as any to insert this, because it needs to be said. Getting on a plane and heading off to combat is not as hard as it may seem. The really hard part was kissing my two small children, ages two and newborn, goodnight, not knowing when I would ever see them again. Then my wife and I retreated to our bedroom and spent one last

CHAPTER 8: PERSIAN GULF WAR

night together until I had to get up and get dressed, kiss her on the cheek, while I whispered to her that I loved her, and turn and walk away and out the door of our apartment. I walked all the way to the unit that morning so I could have myself a good cry and get over it in time to be the sergeant and leader I had to be to my men.

For the next few weeks we spent our time training, waiting for our vehicles to arrive at port so we could get them painted desert camouflage, then get them loaded and ready to move toward the front lines. I do not now remember why, but for some reason, either they ran out of paint, or we just ran out of time, our vehicle never got painted and was a large green glob in a sandy desert environment (it stuck out like a sore thumb.) Finally on January 16th we were all loaded up onto semi-trucks to haul us one hundred miles north toward Iraq the next day. That night was when the air battle started with a bombardment of Bagdad and many strategic targets throughout Iraq. I remember this because we were ordered to put on our chemical suits except for our mask and gloves in preparedness of a counter attack. There were men out guarding the vehicles that did not receive that order so I commandeered the first sergeant's hummer and drove out to give them that order. As I arrived and shut off the hummer to get out, all of a sudden the whole sky above me lit up with lights everywhere, as the first sortie of bombers was returning to base to land and they turned on their landing lights. The sky went from black to pure light in just a flicker of a second. What an impressive sight to behold. That was just the first of many things I would behold during my tour of combat.

The next day we moved forward to our drop off point and from there we were on our own. There were times when the food we were being served was also our enemy (because it was spoiled) and then there were times that we did not get any food or water for days on end and wished we had some of that spoiled food. Then on the thirteenth of February our unit was ordered up to within five miles of Iraq to support a team of scouts that was going to enter and do their job. They located several targets and called in support, so we lit their candle and let them have it with all nine cannons we had in our battery. As the saying goes, "There is no NORMAL response to war." Some of the soldiers began to shout and jump around like it was New Year's Eve and they were having a great time. Others just sat there like they were in shock, but for me, I lay in my foxhole weeping as I knew that maybe not all, but for the most part, the men we would be fighting would be Muslim, and that meant that those who had just died, did so without knowing Jesus Christ as their Saviour, which means that they would split

CHAPTER 8: PERSIAN GULF WAR

hell wide open. I might as well say this now and I will probably say it again later, but the worst thing for a soldier is, not to die for his country, it is to do so and then spend eternity in the torments of HELL. Why should I weep over my enemy?

Matthew 5:43-44 *"Ye have heard that it hath been said, Thou shalt love thy neighbour, and hate thine enemy. But I say unto you, Love your enemies, bless them that curse you, do good to them that hate you, and pray for them which despitefully use you, and persecute you;"*

Romans 5:8 *"But God commendeth his love toward us, in that, while we were yet sinners, Christ died for us."*

Our next engagement was not until the twenty-fourth of February when the "ground war" officially began. We were told to be prepared for up to nine hours of continuous fire and so we were prepared, but our missions were called short that day because our fire was so precise that we knocked out all enemy targets in our sector within just a few hours. As we began moving forward into the areas we had just shelled, we began to see the devastation we had caused on the enemy encampments. It was still dark outside as we began setting up our defenses at one location, when all of a sudden the captain's voice came over his loudspeaker, and he turned on his headlights as he shouted, "Everyone back into your vehicles, we are in a mine field." We were blessed of the Lord as the worst injury was a piece of shrapnel that grazed one soldier's leg when a mine went off near him. One of my soldiers was digging his foxhole when he scooped up a clump of dirt and tossed it aside, only to find out that it too contained a land mine that exploded upon impact and grazed him just a little. Later that morning, after the sun came up, we got back out and surveyed the damage. It was then that I noticed my heel print in the sand from the night before. You see, I was a sergeant, and believed in leading my men in battle. Thus, I was the first one out of the vehicle that night, and if our vehicle had rolled just four inches further ahead of where it was, I would have stepped directly on one of those mines as I exited the vehicle. Why it did not explode as near to it as I stepped is unknown to me other than to say God just did not want it that way.

2 Samuel 22:37 *"Thou hast enlarged my steps under me; so that my feet did not slip."*

There are so many stories like this that I could tell but that is not the point of this book; it is to emphasize to the reader that God had this all planned out and allowed me to live through combat for a reason. Finding that reason is the subject and title to yet

CHAPTER 8: PERSIAN GULF WAR

another chapter of my life and for a long time something that was difficult to understand. See page 185 for the Gospel Tract "Battle Ready Sir" which is one of the things that came out of this.

CHAPTER NINE
Finding A Reason

It is not the battles, nor is it the number of sights that we had to endure that hardens the soldier; it is when the humanity inside you begins to erode away and you no longer care if you live or if you die; you just want it to end. The longer you are in battle, the more desensitized you become, and soon you could care less about life or death. You don't want medals, or recognition, you only want to do your job and be left alone. We think while in battle, "Man, if I can just get home" but once you get back home you realize that no one there understands you and very few even want to try to understand what you have been through. Once you have seen the depravity of what man is capable of in war you begin to question everything about society and your place in it.

It seems that society thinks when a soldier comes home from combat that it is a time of celebration, and I guess there should be that aspect of it. But what so few are able to comprehend, let alone understand, is that coming home is probably the most difficult part of combat. Family and friends are happy that you have returned home; even if there are injuries there is still an excitement to welcome the soldier home. However, it is impossible for anyone who has never been there to understand the emotions that overwhelm you from day to day even though you know your tour is over.

Upon my arrival home, some very good friends of ours had asked us over for a cookout to celebrate my safe return home. They invited several people from our church and other soldiers from their unit to be there and enjoy the fun, food, and fellowship of that afternoon. My wife, children and I arrived and joined them in their living room while the host continued to cook the meal. At one point my friend put a new movie into the VCR player, not understanding what was about to take place. The film was about the Civil War so he never gave it a thought, but as the fighting scenes began to intensify, it struck a shallow nerve in my soul and I had to get out of that room. Not completely understanding why, I began to weep uncontrollably as I ran to find a place to be alone. It took them nearly an hour to find me huddled down in the basement of their building in a combative state of mind. My friend had no intentions of causing me such pain, nor did he realize that the movie he put in would cause me to have flashbacks and nightmares that night, but that is exactly my point; that even when we arrive back home with our friends and families, we are still not home. Our minds will forever relive the events of combat and play upon our emotions, causing us to

CHAPTER 9: FINDING A REASON

sometimes be withdrawn from others. Often this is misinterpreted, that we are anti-social or untrusting, but really has very little, if anything, to do with that. The real reason for it stems from the battles within our minds and how we must learn to live with what we had to do, as well as the curse of the nightmare.

Before you, the reader, goes any further, please let me state for the record that this chapter, let alone this entire book, is not a plea for your sympathy. There is no desire here for sympathy nor pity. NEVER have I held or intended to give the impression "feel sorry for me I'm a combat veteran" although many times I have been accused of it. Remarks like that only further deepen the void of understanding in the life of a soldier. This kind of thinking only drives soldiers further into an empty shell, which is exactly what happened to our Vietnam brothers. We don't expect you to understand what we have been through, we simply desire for you to accept us for who we have become and respect the process that brought us to this point. There has never been a man (or woman for that matter) who has had the privilege of experiencing combat that ever came home the same. The person who left home never comes home again. That person dies in battle and we are forever changed by it. Yes, we come back in the same flesh that we left in, but our hearts, minds and even our souls, are completely changed forever. Now back to the story.

After returning home to Germany where we had been deployed from, I received new orders transferring me to Fort Sill, Oklahoma and within just a few weeks we (my wife, children and I) found ourselves back in the good ol' U.S. of A., driving across the country to my new duty station. While stationed there I had many doors of opportunity opened to me that would have advanced my career in the Army, but I was trying to understand what God was doing in my life and why I had to endure the hardship of combat. Even though while I was over in Iraq and Kuwait I had the privilege of leading two young soldiers to the Lord, I still needed to make sense of it all. I was offered a chance to go to the board for staff sergeant as well as attend the next NCO school that I needed to get that promotion, but God kept impressing upon my heart that neither of those was his plan for my life. I wanted to stay in the Army at this point, but God kept knocking upon my heart saying, "This is not where I want you." I struggled with this for over six months and counseled with my pastor about it many times. Finally one day as I was sitting in my truck in the parking lot of my unit early in the morning and was praying about this matter, I remember it as if God was seated right there next to me in the truck. I expressed to the Lord the opportunities that I had as an NCO in

CHAPTER 9: FINDING A REASON

the military, and how they needed a good godly man like myself in these ungodly line units, until God said to me, "If you want to stay, then do so as you will go far, but this is not the plan I have for your life." That statement took all the argumentation out of me and I submitted to God's will.

Although I had just reenlisted a little over a year before for another three years, the Army came out with a "volunteer out" after Desert Storm was finished. I had only been at Fort Sill for about six months but knew God wanted me out so I submitted my application to get out. Our unit then deployed to Fort Irwin, California for a month to do some more desert training and while we were there they closed that opening to get out. I had no way of knowing whether or not my application had been accepted and had to wait on pins and needles until we returned to Fort Sill that next month before I could check on my status.

Once we were back at Fort Sill, I obtained permission from our first sergeant to visit the division personal office and check on my status. When I told the staff sergeant who was working there how I had put in for the volunteer out, but was then deployed away from the unit for a month, he was kind enough to help me look into my status. He pulled up a list of names on his computer of those who had been approved before the window had closed. He began searching page by page and just kept hitting the next page button, finally looking at me and saying, "Well sergeant, I don't think you made it because there are only a few pages left." Yet he kept hitting the next page button. Finally the last page came up and there it was. Yes, my name was the next to the last one on the list. The Army was looking to get about thirty thousand soldiers to volunteer out and there were over thirty-three thousand just at Fort Sill that took advantage of this early out. I had been praying while I was still in California that if God wanted me out He would have to get my name on that list, and that He did.

1Peter 4:2 *"That he no longer should live the rest of his time in the flesh to the lusts of men, but to the will of God"*.

Just a few weeks later I was out-processing from the military life I loved so much, headed to Michigan with my wife and two children; no job, no place to live, and no idea of what God wanted for my life.

CHAPTER TEN

Enter The Ministry

Once again I must backtrack a little to make sure everything is in its proper perspective. I was saved in August of nineteen eighty and then one year later felt the call of God on my life to preach. It was about that time in my life that I experienced some very trying times and for the second time someone whom I had allowed to be very close to me did me wrong and this made me bitter against everyone including God. Why is it that when men do us wrong we blame God? Although I have always had a desire to serve our nation in the military, when I joined the Army it was not just patriotism, it was also an attempt to run from God's calling upon my life.

Psalm 139:7-14 "Whither shall I go from thy spirit? or whither shall I flee from thy presence? (8) If I ascend up into heaven, thou art there: if I make my bed in hell, behold, thou art there. (9) If I take the wings of the morning, and dwell in the uttermost parts of the sea; (10) Even there shall thy hand lead me, and thy right hand shall hold me. (11) If I say, Surely the darkness shall cover me; even the night shall be light about me. (12) Yea, the darkness hideth not from thee; but the night shineth as the day: the darkness and the light are both alike to thee. (13) For thou hast possessed my reins: thou hast covered me in my mother's womb. (14) I will praise thee; for I am fearfully and wonderfully made: marvellous are thy works; and that my soul knoweth right well".

After getting right with God soon after entering the Army, I still had a lot to learn about God and His Word. My wife and I attended the Divarty Chapel on post, which had a Baptist chaplain who helped me in my young Christian life. However it was not until the Lord gave me orders (through the Army of course) to move to Baumholder, Germany that my calling was to be renewed by God. After arriving in Baumholder, we were invited to attend Grace Baptist Church by another soldier (who is now a pastor himself) as he gave me a ride onto post one morning. We visited there that next Sunday morning only to find out that they were having a special preacher all week long that week, so we decided to attend every meeting that we could. By the end of the week we knew that we should join this church and at that point God renewed His call upon my life to preach His Word. I was never so scared in my life, but knew that I must obey His call. Therefore this time there was no hesitation as I submitted to that call, not knowing that it would still be several years before He could get me back to where he wanted me to be. For the next three years I was

CHAPTER 10: ENTER THE MINISTRY

taught and trained by my Pastor, Dr. Tim Clark, as he took a mixed-up kid and slowly but methodically showed and taught me one Biblical doctrine after another. There were many deployments which interrupted this training and even my tour in Desert Storm, but this is where I was grounded in the Word of God. I hold Brother Clark in very high esteem as he was my Paul to his student Timothy (me). God used this man to influence many a young man and, as of the writing of this book, there are still seventeen of us in full-time Christian work.

After leaving Germany we spent just a little under a year in Lawton, Oklahoma where we started a children's ministry at the small church we joined there. During those few months we were able to lead at least eight young children to the Lord through our puppet ministry that we did every Sunday evening. It was while we were in Oklahoma that God called me out of the service and directed us back to Michigan, to the little town where my wife had grown up. As I ended the last chapter, we moved there with two small children, no job and no place to live, so my in-laws took us in and allowed us to live in their basement (which was set up like a one bedroom apartment). We stayed there for four months while I found work and a place of our own for us to live and raise our family. God was at work in all of that as I helped build the apartment that we ended up renting, but while we were building it the owner already had someone else signed up to rent it. Upon its completion that renter backed out of the contract (unannounced to us) as we both went up to the Church to pray for God to give us a place to live. The very next morning at Church the owner came up to me and asked if we would like to rent his apartment. Never question what God is doing, just allow Him to work in His timing.

Upon arrival in my wife's home town we visited a small Baptist Church there as we had done many times while home on leave. The pastor was excited to see us and within just a few weeks asked me to be his Youth and Assistant Pastor. It was a volunteer position but I was beginning to see God's hand in leading us there and what it was that he wanted me to do. We served there for over three years, impacting and leading many young souls to Jesus Christ. During that same time God gave us a house of our own that we were able to remodel and then sell making a small profit as He once again added to my calling. Shortly after getting our house finished the Lord again directed me to talk to my pastor about being a full-time youth pastor. I knew that our Church could not afford such a position, but in obedience to God, I made an appointment to speak with my pastor, not telling him what it was about, but that I needed some counseling on a particular matter.

CHAPTER 10: ENTER THE MINISTRY

Later that week we met and as I entered into his office he asked me to sit down just as the phone rang, so I sat down and he answered the phone. I could not help but overhear the conversation he was having with another pastor on the phone and could not believe what I was hearing either. Finally he ended the phone conversation with, "Well Pastor, I will keep my ears open and if I hear of anyone who is looking for full time position, I will let you know." He hung up the phone while looking at me and said, "So what do you want to talk to me about?" After sitting there for just a quick moment, taking it all in, I looked at my pastor and began telling him how God had been speaking to me about serving Him full time and how I knew that our church was not in a position to do that, so I just wanted to ask him to pray about it with me. My pastor then picked up the phone and called Pastor Petty back and said, "You're not going to believe this but...." as he relayed my story over the phone. That meeting was in October and by February of the New Year, God had moved us down to a suburb of Detroit as their full time Youth Pastor and the Assistant Pastor of the Church.

We purchased a house that was only a few miles from the church, so from time to time I would ride my bicycle to the church and then use one of the church vehicles to run errands if need be. Only a few weeks after starting this new position, I was riding my bicycle to the church one morning as a car ran a stop sign and broadsided my bicycle, tossing me up on the hood of the car. Other than being shocked, I was not in any pain until the driver chose to put her car into reverse and back suddenly away from the accident, tossing me off of her hood and onto my damaged bicycle. When I showed up late for the office that morning my pastor asked why I was not there on time. As I explained he just said "Oh, so you're the reason for the ambulance out here." The accident happened in front of the parking lot next to our church and was just outside of the pastor's office window. A few months later as I was approaching the last intersection before reaching the church, a car from the oncoming lane made a left turn across the path of my pickup truck. This was not a problem but behind her was another car that made the same turn without looking to see if the way was clear as I broadsided her car. I had to react quickly to avoid being tossed towards oncoming traffic and fortunately, no one was seriously injured. Just thought I should share these two incidences so you would not think that my life-threatening days were over. Oh yes, there was another just after taking this position. We were still living up near my wife's home town and I was commuting back and forth down state. One morning when I awoke, it was a half hour later than what I had set the alarm for and it never went off. I quickly washed up, got dressed, and jumped into our

CHAPTER 10: ENTER THE MINISTRY

car to get on the road as quickly as possible. It was a little over a two hour drive if the traffic was not bad, but today it was going to be worse than bad. After only about thirty minutes on I-75 South, a state police car came flying past me, followed by another and yet another county sheriff's car. Just a few miles up the road they had the whole expressway blocked off and there we sat for over an hour. Finally they escorted us across the Saginaw River and forced us to exit on the first exit, directing us to go through downtown Saginaw before we could again get back on the highway. I had already called my pastor and let him know that I was in a traffic jam and did not know when I would get there, but he said not to worry about it, just get here as soon as I safely could. Finally I arrived down in Livonia at the church, only three hours late. I was there to do my work for that day and then head to stay with a friend who would put me up through the week. While sitting there in my friend's home that night, eating supper, we were watching the news on TV. That is when I discovered why I had been so late getting to the church that morning. There had been a bank robbery just north of where my wife and I were living and it quickly became a race down the highway, ending up in a shootout right around the Saginaw area. The state police had chased them and exchanged gun fire all the way down the interstate highway. If I had gotten up when I had set the alarm and left, I would have been right in the middle of that pursuit. Sometimes we just do not know how much God is protecting us and our families, and then sometimes He lets us see later just what He did for us.

> Psalm 28:7 *"The LORD is my strength and my shield; my heart trusted in him, and I am helped: therefore my heart greatly rejoiceth; and with my song will I praise him."*

Once again this man of God that was put into my life taught me and trained me, this time in administration. He taught me how to work with people and how to get them to work with you. He taught me the things you don't learn in Bible College, like how to plant a bush or a tree, when to pull up a dead one, and when to just give it a little tender loving care. You say what does this have to do with ministry? Well, people are like plants and there are some that just need to be uprooted, but you had better understand that their roots may cause problems with other plants that are nearby and inadvertently uproot those plants as well. Sometimes it is better just to nurse them back to health so that all around them see what God has done.

> Matthew 13:24-30 *"Another parable put he forth unto them, saying, The kingdom of heaven is likened unto a man which sowed good seed in his field: (25) But while men*

CHAPTER 10: ENTER THE MINISTRY

slept, his enemy came and sowed tares among the wheat, and went his way. (26) But when the blade was sprung up, and brought forth fruit, then appeared the tares also. (27) So the servants of the householder came and said unto him, Sir, didst not thou sow good seed in thy field? from whence then hath it tares? (28) He said unto them, An enemy hath done this. The servants said unto him, Wilt thou then that we go and gather them up? (29) But he said, Nay; lest while ye gather up the tares, ye root up also the wheat with them. (30) Let both grow together until the harvest: and in the time of harvest I will say to the reapers, Gather ye together first the tares, and bind them in bundles to burn them: but gather the wheat into my barn."

Pastor H. L. Petty taught me how to love people regardless of how they love you. There is more to leading a flock of people than getting them to do what you want; a good shepherd leads the flock to do what his Father in Heaven wants. When I have studied about shepherds, one thing that I have noticed is that a shepherd leads his flock and they will follow. A shepherd who tries to push his flock causes them to scatter.

John 10:27 *"My sheep hear my voice, and I know them, and they follow me:"*

Over the next five years I was taught many things but if I had to sum them all up into one it would be this:

Jude 1:22 *"And of some have compassion, making a difference:"*

The last thing that Pastor Petty taught me was how to say goodbye. As he lay sick in the hospital with cancer he asked me to step up and do a funeral for a family in our church. That one funeral turned into five funerals in just as many weeks and then, shortly thereafter, it was Pastor Petty's turn to go home to be with the Lord. I have never gotten over the influence of this one man who taught me so much about God. I will never forget him or his love for the Lord and the lost.

The year that Pastor Petty died was very difficult for the church and especially for his wife and family. We had always done our own youth camp every summer and there were some in the church that said we should just forgo it for one year, but I argued the point that Pastor Petty would not want it that way. As a matter of fact, he lived all year long to see young people come to know Jesus Christ as Saviour and that was always the highlight of that one week of camp. So

CHAPTER 10: ENTER THE MINISTRY

with that settled we continued with the already made plans for our youth camp, minus Pastor Petty. Every day as time would draw closer to camp starting something seemed different, and it was, but finally that day came and after loading up the buses we headed out to Camp Bethel. Although we had to drive through rain all the way there, by the time we arrived at the campground it was in a downpour, so we had to sit on the buses for over an hour before it let up enough for everyone to get off and move their belongings to their cabins. That night during a huge thunderstorm a tree fell and took out the electricity for the whole camp. With no electricity, we also would not have any water as it was from a well and needed electricity to run the pump.

Once again we found ourselves in a quandary as to what to do. Several of the staff wanted to just pack up and go back home, but many of the children's parents had put them in camp and then went away for the week, so even if we went back to the church, we still had to come up with a plan on what to do with all the kids. After praying about it we decided to stick it out. One of the men and I each had F-250s so we took one and went back to town to get a generator and fresh water for drinking. We purchased eight large plastic garbage cans and filled them with water for cooking and drinking and hauled them back to the camp. We parked his truck and took mine as we went back to town to pick up barbeques and propane to run them, as well as many other items that we were asked to pick up. We did this over and over, switching out trucks, picking up supplies, and driving them back and forth for three days until the power came back on. On that forth day, during chapel, we had several young people accept Jesus Christ as their Saviour, which made it all worthwhile. That night the two of us, who had been running supplies, finally got a night's sleep just in time to bus all the kids back home at the end of the last day, Friday.

Three months later we understood the importance of sticking it out at camp that year as a tragedy took place with one of the families who had sent their children to camp. Early in the morning their house had caught on fire due to an electric heater being too close to the curtains in the living room. One of those young boys who had received Jesus Christ as his Saviour that summer made it as far as the landing right in front of the front door before collapsing and dying from smoke inhalation. What if we would have cancelled camp that year because we were mourning over our deceased Pastor? What if we had gone back to the Church and he would have gone home instead of hearing his need of a Saviour? We did not have to consider the "what if's," we already understood that

CHAPTER 10: ENTER THE MINISTRY

God was in the middle of it all. What a consolation that we could go to that grieving mother and tell her about her son's decision during camp. It did not bring her son back, nor did it immediately remove her pain, but over a year later she told me that it was a comfort to know he was in a better place.

The passing of Pastor Petty shook me pretty hard to say the least. I floundered for several years, not in my faith, but wondering where God wanted me to go from there. One day as I was attending a preachers meeting, one of the pastors there addressed the crowd, speaking of his need for a youth pastor. I approached him during the fellowship dinner that followed and introduced myself as someone who was interested in the position. We spoke at length that day and then he had me bring my family over to his home on several occasions as we further discussed his need and got better acquainted with each other.

After much prayer he decided that I should come to the church and candidate for the open position, and then he would discuss this with his deacons. While there that day we went out to eat, and as we were dining, a couple at the table next to us asked if we were both preachers, to which we replied, "Yes." They in turn handed us a paper about their church celebrating its third anniversary and invited us to the meetings that started on Saturday with preaching, singing, and food.

ALLOWED TO LIVE

We thanked them and continued about our business of fellowshipping and finishing our meal. That evening the pastor met with his deacons and they voted against me coming there as the youth pastor, which left him in quite a frustrated position as he had set his heart on us being there. He later told me that he could have gone ahead and hired me, but he was getting ready to retire and did not want to cause problems for either of us in the future. Just before the evening service he called me into the office and broke the news to me and could tell that it was upsetting to us as well. But I had learned that if God is not in it, do not push it. So I thanked him for the opportunity and went out into the auditorium singing and preaching that night as if nothing was wrong. That pastor was amazed at my attitude and we have remained good friends ever since.

That next Saturday was the third anniversary of the church we had been invited to, so I asked him if he was going, and he said yes, so my wife, children and I met him and his wife there on Saturday and sat with them during the meeting. Although I had kept a cool head that Sunday evening I was hurting inside and really in need of a huge blessing, but my spirit was one of "bless me if you can" as I sat there that morning. Then it happened; a singing group from down in South Carolina sang a song about more grace, and my heart began to melt, ever so slightly, but it was warming up.

CHAPTER 10: ENTER THE MINISTRY

After they sang, the pastor and host of the meeting introduced the next preacher and he preached on "More Grace." Now I was in a mess. God used that man to show me that my heart was cold because of all the hurt my family and I had been through since the passing of our pastor several years back, and God had brought it to a head there and then. By the time brother Pelky finished preaching I was a sobbing mess. God had moved into the open seat next to me and just put his loving arms around me and loved on me while he preached. I had never before experienced the presence of Almighty God the way I did that day and knew that God was leading us to unite with that church. We visited there for the next several weeks and then finally joined during their first "Camp Meeting," which was held in the parking lot of a strip mall where the church was located. Just as in the past God had shown his direction for me, and once again I knew we were in God's perfect will for our lives.

We were members of that church for nearly a year before Pastor McCoy asked me to be his youth pastor. Of course I accepted the opportunity to, once again, work with the teens and young adults, leading them to trust Christ, not just for salvation, but also with their daily lives. I had never met a man like Dr. McCoy, although when he and Dr. Clark got together, they were two peas in a pod and I was cooked toast between the two of them. I've never been picked on so much by two people whom I love so dearly, and that is what made it all fun and encouraging.

During those first two to three years, as well as the years that have followed, this man of God led me to begin to understand how to follow the leadership of the Holy Ghost of God. As God would move in our lives he would point that out to me, and as God would move in the Church, we became sensitive to that movement and watched as God was glorified for what He was doing, and not a particular man for what involvement that man had invested. Yes, my life was once again tested as we were decorating our new Church building for our fourth anniversary. I was on a ladder hanging banners all around the church exterior when the ladder collapsed and I came tumbling to the ground, landing flat on my back with my leg still caught up in what was left of the ladder, which gave me quite a jolt as it stretched my knee. Several of the men that were there that day rushed to my side but in just a few hours I was up and walking around, a little sore and bruised but still in the fight. However, I am now banned from using a ladder ever again! (Alas, but I have had to ignore that ban from time to time.) Shortly after that fall the pastor asked me to step down from being the youth pastor and asked if I would head up the correspondence Bible College that he had

CHAPTER 10: ENTER THE MINISTRY

started. That night and throughout that week I prayed about this change of life for me and felt that God was moving me in that direction. So the next week I resigned as youth pastor and took the position as dean in the college. I still love to work with youth and probably always will, but looking back on this move one can definitely see the hand of Almighty God and how he used Dr. Tim McCoy as my pastor to both lead and teach me to follow the Holy Ghost of God. Although that church is no longer in existence, the things learned there under the tutelage of that man of God will forever be with me. He has become like my own father and an extraordinarily good friend and brother in Christ. God used him to get us to the point we are today in the ministry that He (God) had been preparing us for.

I pray that anyone who is reading this book that you would learn what I learned in how important it is to fully submit to those in authority over you. Not just because they watch for your soul, but because you cannot achieve the level or position of authority that God wants to take you to, until you submit to those whom God places over you. I have often said that if there were ever issues that came up between my pastor and me, that no one else would ever know it. When those times would occur (and they did) I would simply take the matter to our Lord and Saviour. After all, God is our Father and it is his responsibility to correct His children. Sometimes it meant that he would correct our pastor, but often times it meant that he had to correct me.

CHAPTER ELEVEN

Bible College Is Important

As a youth pastor one of the things I was asked all the time was; "Where did you go to Bible College?" I would always respond by telling them about how I was trained while in Germany and left it at that. To be brutally honest, I felt that time was too short for me to spend four years cooped up in a Bible college when there were souls that needed to be led to Christ. After all, I had been taught the doctrines of Jesus Christ, so what more was there to learn? When we started attending Liberty Baptist Church in Belleville, Michigan, it was brought to my attention that they had a Bible college. Since it did not interfere with my job or the time I spent soul winning and such, I would endeavor to complete my degree and get some education.

During my time in the Army I had taken correspondence courses from Trinity Baptist Bible College in Jacksonville, Florida through the church we were in while in Germany. After moving back to Michigan I took some correspondence courses through Liberty University, but that did not last long either as doctrine became an issue that was unavoidable. Then while living in the Detroit area, I learned about

Midwestern Bible College and finished my Associate degree there. However, because of distance and financial burdens, I decided not to pursue any further degrees until the Lord opened another door, and that is just what he did through Liberty Baptist Bible College and Theological Seminary. As a member of Liberty Baptist Church, we could attend the Bible College free of any expense, so that too was very interesting to me. Please do not misunderstand me as being cheap, but rather, I had been unemployed for several years and had a bunch of bills that I was trying to get caught up and paid off, so funds were very few to say the least.

Within just a very short time I had completed the required studies for my bachelor's degree and with that in hand, Pastor McCoy encouraged me to press on for a master's degree. He explained that he had been observing how thorough I had been in my studies and said that he wanted me to consider becoming the Dean of Academics for the Bible College, but in order to do that I needed at least a master's degree. So again I hit the books, as they say, and began my studies toward having a master's degree. Although it was challenging, studying has always been something that I have been good at. I enjoyed the process of learning more than I ever thought there was to learn about the Bible and the truths taught in it.

I was growing leaps and bounds in the faith as my

CHAPTER 11: BIBLE COLLEGE IS IMPORTANT

education continued. Within less than a year I received my master's degree and the appointment as the Dean of Academics for Liberty Baptist Bible College. Perhaps you, the reader, may be wondering why all of a sudden I had become so interested in a Bible Education, and that is a fair question. What drew me to this school was not just that as a member of our church there was no cost for tuition, but it was the philosophy that this institution has towards students from other churches. Here is a quote from our brochure:

> "Liberty Baptist Bible College and Theological Seminary is one that supports the Biblical Christian approach to higher education without removing the student from their Local New Testament Baptist Church.
>
> We believe that this approach provides students with the best possible programs to achieve their education, while they continue to support and build the Local Work where God has placed them."

At the Founding of Liberty Baptist Bible College and Theological Seminary, Dr. McCoy had the intentions of making this a college where students could study God's Word no matter where they were located in the world. He also desired to establish a campus for students in the local area to be able to attend as well. However it was never his intent to pull someone out of another Biblical church to build a college, and quite frankly, I liked that.

You may think that the promotion I received was a prestigious thing, and at first it was, for about one week. Then I realized the work that needed to be done to make this a successful college for training young Christian minds for the ministry. Although our curriculum was some of the best that is out there (so I have been told) it was not available in a format that was easily useable beyond our church campus. One of my first tasks was to take the material we had and make it digital (that means putting it into a computer for you non-computer types out there). That process took several years as I was also working a full time job on the side, you know to pay my bills and such. Then there were the records that needed to be updated. However, before that could be done we had to develop a system that would catalog all our courses on a computer and also work in creating record files. This task again took me a very long time to perfect, but due to several injuries at work, I had several months off of work and spent that time completing this task. It was simply a matter of developing an alpha-numeric system, and that has worked great. Every course is assigned a six digit code; the first three digits are

CHAPTER 11: BIBLE COLLEGE IS IMPORTANT

letters letting us know what degree program it is from and the last three digits are numbers letting us know what course it is in that degree study. With this now completed, it was time to introduce our record keeping to the twenty-first century.

All the previous work was done so that I could build a program that would keep track of what classes a student had taken. We also wanted it to track grades for those classes, and automatically produce a transcript of each student's education anytime it would be requested. After several days of working on this program and trying to get it to produce a transcript, it finally worked. My wife thought I was nuts, loony, bonkers, you know, just lost it, as I started shouting and jumping around the room. It had taken me nearly five years of planning, thinking things through, and labor, to finally achieve this goal. IT WORKED, IT WORKED, IT WORKED!!! I was so excited that it finally worked. I called Dr. McCoy and began to share with him how the Lord had helped me with the programming so that now our transcripts would be automatic, which made his day. Even though it initiated a great deal of work, with great joy I began to transfer all of our students records onto this new program one by one. Of course you know that as I would finish each student's records I would pull up the transcript and just look at it already filled in.

ALLOWED TO LIVE

As I look back upon my life I never had envisioned that I would be involved in education. Then again, upon taking a second look, my mother was a school teacher and principal in the public school system. She had taught me my ABC's, how to read, and some arithmetic before I ever entered kindergarten. Although I did not always carry the best grades in school, when I did put an effort into studying it was easy to get A's & B's. In college I was often looked to by fellow students for assistance on the materials we were studying. In the military, to be a leader, you must first become a student. As an NCO (Non-Commissioned Officer) we were always called upon to prepare and execute training lessons on various subjects in our MOS (Military Occupation) as well as disseminate common military knowledge. Upon leaving the military I was asked to help build a Christian School, (not just the building but running the school,) and was made the principal for the first year of its operation. In youth ministry I taught classes on Wednesday evening and during Sunday school and yet again during our Friday Night Youth Club. Was it such a leap to then become the Dean of a Bible College and a professor of that same school? No, upon looking at it closer, I believe that God knew what He was doing and prepared me for this position in my life.

CHAPTER 11: BIBLE COLLEGE IS IMPORTANT

Mat 28:18-20 *"And Jesus came and spake unto them, saying, All power is given unto me in heaven and in earth. (19) Go ye therefore, and teach all nations, baptizing them in the name of the Father, and of the Son, and of the Holy Ghost: (20) Teaching them to observe all things whatsoever I have commanded you: and, lo, I am with you alway, even unto the end of the world. Amen."*

Romans 10:13-15 *"For whosoever shall call upon the name of the Lord shall be saved. (14) How then shall they call on him in whom they have not believed? and how shall they believe in him of whom they have not heard? and how shall they hear without a preacher? (15) And how shall they preach, except they be sent? as it is written, How beautiful are the feet of them that preach the gospel of peace, and bring glad tidings of good things!"*

2Timothy 2:1-5 *"Thou therefore, my son, be strong in the grace that is in Christ Jesus. (2) And the things that thou hast heard of me among many witnesses, the same commit thou to faithful men, who shall be able to teach others also. (3) Thou therefore endure hardness, as a good soldier of Jesus Christ. (4) No man that warreth entangleth himself with the affairs of this life; that he may please him who hath chosen him to be a soldier. (5) And if a man also strive for masteries, yet is he not crowned, except he strive lawfully."*

Should we then desire not only to educate ourselves, but our children, our spouses, and of course our brothers and sisters in Christ? There is however one pitfall that takes place in Christian education. Over the many years and through the broad experiences that I have had the privilege of learning from, I have observed one common misnomer. Just because a man obtains a Bible College degree, that does not make him a preacher! There are too many pulpits today that are filled with "man-made preachers" and not "God called preachers." Our churches are suffering from these men who claim that the Bible is their only life rule of faith and practice, but then place the teachings of their institutions above what the Bible says. Recently I was promoted to the position of President of Liberty Baptist Bible College and Theological Seminary (which is another story for another chapter). Even in this position I still don't believe that obtaining a degree from our institution qualifies you as a pastor. If God's call is not on your life, you may become educated but little else will ever become of it. Bible college in and of itself can never prepare a student to become a pastor. Only when you have the privilege of serving

CHAPTER 11: BIBLE COLLEGE IS IMPORTANT

under a man of God, who will take the time to instruct and train you in ministry, will you then be prepared for what lies ahead. Education is important, and that is why we offer it through correspondence, so a person does not have to leave their church or current job, but they can work on their studies at home as they have time. We encourage our students to take the time they need with their families and if it takes a little longer to finish their studies, then so be it. Yet, education in and of itself is just that: education, knowledge. In order to pastor or even serve in any aspect of ministry one must learn how to take that knowledge and use it wisely. That, my friend, is "Wisdom" which comes from both having a mentor and being a mentor to someone else. The most important lessons I ever learned about the ministry were not taught in "Bible College." They were taught to me by my pastor, mentor, teacher and friend. I have been triply blessed to have had three men in my life who have helped me through this process. There is no doubt that my wife and I are where we are today, doing what we are doing for the Lord, except it first be for the calling of the LORD and then for those men who guided and directed me into truth, knowledge and of course, wisdom.

> Proverbs 4:5-7 *"Get wisdom, get understanding: forget it not; neither decline from the words of my mouth. (6) Forsake her*

not, and she shall preserve thee: love her, and she shall keep thee. (7) Wisdom is the principal thing; therefore get wisdom: and with all thy getting get understanding."

CHAPTER TWELVE

Operation Liberty

Everything you have read so far leads up to this ministry! Everything! Every trial, every blessing, everything herein contained, GOD used to bring us to the place He wanted us to be!!!

> Romans 8:28 *"And we know that all things work together for good to them that love God, to them who are the called according to his purpose."*

Do you remember back in chapter two where I shared with you all of my "Mountain Top Experiences"? Well, this is one of those in a spiritual sense then. As we are climbing the mountain we can see little but the dirt and rocks that are directly in front of us. Even if we dare take a glance from side to side, there is little more than dirt, rocks and vegetation to see. However, once we reach the summit of the mountain we can clearly see just where we started and the path of our entire journey as we made our way up that mountain. This chapter then, is as I am standing on the summit of my life and looking back. It is easy now to see how God used every aspect of the things I have endured in my life to bring me to the point He wanted me to be. In the deepest and darkest times of

ALLOWED TO LIVE

our lives we often look to God and question (in our hearts if not out loud), "Do you really care? God, are you even there? Lord, can you not hear my prayers?" It is now from this mountain top perspective that we can see. Yes, the Lord does care, and that He was with us all the time, listening to our every word as He guided and protected us from harm.

During the summer of two thousand five my wife and I were getting ready to attend a "Camp Meeting" at a local Baptist Church that evening, but things were just not going well, and we ended up arriving there late that night. Not real late, but they had already started singing and I DON'T LIKE BEING LATE!!! I wanted to get there early so we could get seats next to our pastor who was also supposed to be there that night, but alas, that did not happen because of arriving so late. Instead we were handed two chairs and the usher took us to the back of one of the middle rows and placed our chairs there behind an elderly man and his wife. At the end of the next song the pastor asked for folks to welcome those around them, so the gentlemen in front of us turned around introducing himself and his wife. He said, "Hi, my name is Dusty Russell and this is my wife, Sandy." Then I replied, "Well, that will be easy enough to remember as my first name is Russell," and then introduced my wife as well. Dusty then spouted that he had spent twenty-six years in the

CHAPTER 12: OPERATION LIBERTY

Army and was a retired warrant officer. To which I let him know that I had spent five years, nine months, eleven days, eight and a half hours in the Army. We both began to laugh and right away enjoyed each other's company. As the preacher began to preach that night, Dusty kept turning around wanting to speak to me, so finally I told him I would be more than happy to stay afterwards as long as he liked to talk if he would just turn around and listen to the preacher. To my surprise that is exactly what Dusty did for the rest of the service.

When the invitation was given I leaned forward and just barely taking hold of Dusty's arm, asked if he wanted to go forward. With no hesitation he said, "Youbetcha" and jumped up out of his chair and started down the aisle with me in fast pursuit. Half way to the alter he turned around motioning to his wife and then said, "Are you coming with me?" She quickly joined us as we made our way down to the altar that night. Dusty knelt down there and began to just pour his heart out to the LORD, begging the Lord to forgive him and save his soul. I just knelt there beside him and prayed for him as he settled things with God. Finally I asked him if he were to die tonight would he know where he would spend eternity, and he shouted, "YOUBETCHA!" With tears running down his cheeks he said, "For the first time I now know that heaven is my home and Jesus is my Saviour."

Four days later I went and visited Dusty at his home where he was tinkering in his work shop. On the one wall were many medals, plaques, military awards, and even a propeller off of one of his airplanes from WWII. As I stood there admiring his wall I said to him, "Man, Dusty, that is some wall of Honor." He just looked at me with tears in his eyes and said, "That was sending me to HELL!" He went on to explain that he thought for years that because he had done so much good in his life, as both a soldier and a man, that he was good enough to go to heaven. It wasn't until he had paid attention to an old-fashioned preacher, under an old-fashioned tent, preaching the old gospel story from an old-fashioned Bible, that Jesus was the only way to heaven, that he knew those awards were not going to get him there. Over the next few months I witnessed many transformations in this man's life as God's gift of salvation began to work in and through him.

Then in the fall of the same year, while preaching a revival in central Michigan, I mentioned my love and respect for our military. That night, two ladies from that church approached me with two boxes of cards that they had made by hand and wanted to send them to soldiers, but did not know how to do that. Knowing several men who have ministries near military bases and to our troops, it was a no-brainer to me. I would

CHAPTER 12: OPERATION LIBERTY

just take the boxes and then divide them up between my friends to give to their soldiers. Within the next few days I was also contacted by a mission board who said they had heard that I wanted to be a missionary to the military. (I had not even spoken to my wife that God was doing something, let alone anyone else.) My brother also called during those few days and told me that he was going back into the Army Reserves. My brother is older than I and had been in for several years before I had ever joined and did not get out until after I had. Now he was telling me that he was going back in and wanted me to pray for him. Then there was the email I received from a friend of mine who is already a missionary to our military in Baumholder, Germany. Brother Steve Meyer had taken over the work there from Dr. Tim Clark and was now the pastor of Grace Baptist Church in Baumholder. In his email he asked if I would consider coming over to Germany and singing at a men's meeting he was hosting for all the Baptist Churches in Europe. All this happened within just a few days, so I just sat back and said, "Ok LORD, what is it that you are doing, and what are you wanting from me? After a night of prayer I booked my tickets for a flight to Germany and said, "Ok Lord, show me what you want and I'll do it."

Well, the trip to Germany wasn't until April of the next year, and it seemed that time sat still as I was eager to make the trip, praying that God would show me what he wanted. I had now told my wife about all the events and had also counseled with my pastor about it several times. He kept encouraging me to keep an open mind and listen for God's direction. Finally the day came for me to board my flight to Germany, and to say that I was excited would be an understatement. I had not been in Germany for over fourteen years and knew that many of the things I remembered would probably be different, and so it was. Although there were some of the same landmarks, everything did appear different, and it seemed surreal that I was once again back in Baumholder. This, after all, was the stomping grounds of where I had first been grounded in the Word of God, so it will always hold a special place in my heart. It was while I was there in Germany that God showed me just what he wanted me to do. As I sat there during the meetings I would observe the folks that Brother Steve was ministering to, and while doing just that, God said to me, "The bases are covered."

The one thing that was drastically different on this trip I noticed when I took a walk around town to see the sights. Once again I passed through the park that had once been a very beautiful and peaceful place to take one's family but it was obvious that it had changed. There were no families there and most of the

CHAPTER 12: OPERATION LIBERTY

areas were overgrown with weeds. It was not the beautiful Germany that I remembered at all. While walking through there, I passed by two young German men who were just sitting on one of the picnic tables. One may never know for sure, but I had the impression that they intended to do me some harm, so as they spoke to me I returned pleasantries to them in my best German and continued on my way. Back at the church I shared this story with Pastor Meyer and he then told me there had been several muggings in that park the last year and it was not a good place to be. I don't know why they did not attack me, or perhaps it was all in my head, but I do know that God protects us often times when we little understand how much trouble we are in.

Upon returning back home to America, I began doing further research about our military bases, and I learned that, in fact, there are good Independent Baptist Churches around all our military bases. However God laid on my heart, "What about your brother?" I researched the National Guard and Reserve and found out that a large portion of our nation's defenses are made up of these soldiers who live and work in rural America. They are not at a "base" but live out in society just like you and I. Upon further investigation I learned that even if there is an armory in your town, that does not mean that those soldiers live in your town; as a matter of fact, we have found that just the opposite is true. Therefore, God showed us that in order to reach these soldiers, we would need to travel from state to state, living on the road if you will, visiting doctrinally sound Baptist churches and teaching them how to reach the National Guard and reservists that live around them.

My wife and I both were working union jobs, and to be honest, we were happy being servants at our local Baptist church where I was also the assistant pastor. As God began to reveal His will to us, at first it was not easy to understand. However our pastor, whom I've mentioned here before, was teaching us how to sense and obey the Holy Ghost of God. We founded Operation Liberty and began sending care packages to soldiers who were deployed and meeting any other needs they would request. At this time my brother was deployed to Iraq and after receiving a care package from us he sent me an email asking if we could get him some fuses for his hummer. That afternoon I went down to the auto parts store and picked up a large box of the fuses that he needed and shipped them to him. When they arrived he wrote me another email and asked if we could get them some squeegees to clean their vehicle windows. You have no idea how dusty it can get over there until you have been there. After talking with the auto parts manager he was able to

CHAPTER 12: OPERATION LIBERTY

donate ten squeegees and then offered to sell as many as we needed at their cost. We took the ten he offered and purchased all the rest of what he had in stock, boxed them up and shipped them to Iraq. My brother was expecting one or two, maybe three, but he was so surprised when he opened the box and saw how many we had shipped. When my brother's unit came home I was able to witness to many of them, passing out tracts and a Gospel CD I had recorded entitled "A HERO." I did not get to witness to them because we had sent tracts, goodies, snacks and other treats to them. I did not get to witness to them because we had shipped New Testaments with a nice military cover and other reading materials. I was able to speak to many of them face to face because, as my brother would take me to each one and introduce me, he would say, "This is who sent us the squeegees." You see, he was expecting only a few, but when he opened the box there was one for each vehicle they had in their unit. I never knew how many vehicles they had but God did. Those squeegees are still ministering to some of them and just last year the Lord gave me a message on the squeegee. We never know what will influence a heart to the Lord but what we are called to do is to be found faithful.

The next miracle that God worked out was putting me in this ministry full time. Up until now I was still working a full time job and trying to minister to the few soldiers we were coming in contact with. Although I had been injured three times in one year at my work, they were still requiring me to do my job regardless of the amount of pain and suffering it caused me. I was getting to the point where I was going to have to make a decision about leaving the job due to the excessive pain and discomfort I was in each day. I had tried to get them to put me in another department that did not require so much lifting and using my injured back, but they would not hear of that other than for a few weeks, and then back to the grind stone for me. As I was sitting in my work truck during our lunch time (that is when I would read my Bible and pray) I began talking with the Lord about how I could not make it much longer and then asked Him if He wanted me in this ministry full time or part time? To my surprise, the answer came the very next day as I was called into the office with my foreman, the personal officer, and union president. They explained that cuts had to be made and that I was being laid off with no known date of return. I was told to turn in all my uniforms, keys and safety equipment by the close of business that day and not to return to work from here on out. Two of the three in the room expressed that they were sorry to cause me such a hardship but this was just simple business, nothing personal. There was also another man laid off the same time as I and

CHAPTER 12: OPERATION LIBERTY

as we both exited the building he was very angry, grumbling and cussing about his predicament. However, as I walked out I just looked to heaven and said, "Ok Lord, if that is what you want, I'll go." I called my pastor and let him know I was laid off and he asked if I wanted to go to North Carolina with him for a meeting in two weeks. I agreed and went home to break the news to my wife.

When my wife got off work I told her what had happened and that I was going to North Carolina with our pastor in two weeks and then reassured her that all would be well. My wife is no novice and she actually was very happy for me and encouraged me to follow the Lord. Two weeks later my pastor, Dr. McCoy, another man from our church, and I piled all our suitcases into a minivan and right after church that night we started heading down to North Carolina. Now before we go any further one must understand something that pastor had said that night while preaching in the evening service. He was making the point that if we were all killed while traveling, then not to weep for us, as we are all saved and would be in heaven. Pastor prayed for our safe travel and we each kissed our wife goodbye prior to leaving. Since I did not mind driving at night, I took the first shift and drove all through that night, getting us most of the way there by the time we stopped for breakfast. Then it was Willie's turn to drive through Virginia, across the mountain and then down into North Carolina. Well, that was the plan anyway, but it did not happen that way. Willie did start driving, but as we started climbing up over the mountain we drove right into a heavy fog. I was so glad that I was no longer driving, but Willie was a nervous wreck. Oops... did I say wreck... yes, that is just what happened as another vehicle pulled out in front of us and Willie did all he could to avoid collision, but, alas, we T-boned her, spinning her around and flinging us off into someone's front yard. Well, to make a long story short we were all fine, just a little bruised from the seat belts, but no other injuries. The woman who pulled out in front of us also was uninjured as well. The real miracle of this ordeal was that the minivan was now a crumpled mess in the front but it was still drivable. Nothing was leaking, squeaking, or rubbing against any other part of the engine. There were no broken parts of the steering column or front wheels. As a matter of fact, we were amazed that it did not pull to one side or the other, nor did it shimmy any at all, but would drive straight down the road even if you let go of the steering wheel. Well, we were SAFE! From that time on we now pray for safe and uneventful travel.

The meeting in North Carolina was supposed to be for just one week but upon our arrival we learned that

CHAPTER 12: OPERATION LIBERTY

it was actually a two-week meeting. Pastor McCoy and Brother Willie were only able to stay for the first week. I fully intended to go home with them but was strongly encouraged by my pastor and the host of the meeting to stay for the second week. My concern was that I had our ministry display, a table, and two bags of materials with me besides my own luggage so I did not know how I was going to get home. It was suggested that I could catch a bus but then I would have to ship all my belonging and did not want to do that. On top of all this I had received a phone call demanding that I return to work that following Monday morning. This just added to the confusion of what I should do. I wanted to stay, but not being sure how I was going to get home weighed heavy on my mind. I continued to pray about it all week and finally decided that perhaps I should stay and leave the getting home part to the Lord. I also made a phone call and terminated my employment. One reason was because I was no longer able to do that kind of physical labor, and the second reason was that God was opening doors for me in North Carolina and, as a preacher, I had to go through them.

The second week of that meeting became a launching pad for our ministry as it opened up to us many other meetings by those with whom we became acquainted that week. I can now see how God used that week as a test to see if I was serious about trusting Him for my needs. The rest of that summer I was invited to many camp meetings around the country and would schedule as many meetings along the way as was possible. God began to bless this trust in Him as a new aspect of our ministry was opened to us. There were many families who began to ask if I would be willing to visit their brother, nephew, cousin and so on. Each time I was requested to visit one of these soldiers, I would inquire as to where they lived, and each time it was directly on the route I was taking to my next meeting. There was no "special" thing I did, but just began visiting these young men and talking to them about how God brought me through the troubles that I had been experiencing. Really all I ever did was to show them that God still loved them and that He still had a plan for their lives. Often times this takes more than one visit, phone call, and follow up. We always try to find a local Baptist church that we can encourage these young men to get involved in. We also have at our disposal the Liberty Baptist Bible College of which we offer our associate degree free of charge to any deployed soldier if they enroll while they are deployed or within one year of their return home. As the president of the Bible College I also have the liberty to extend this to any soldier at any time. Why would we do that? Simply because if we can get a soldier into the Word of God we can then, in turn, get

CHAPTER 12: OPERATION LIBERTY

the Word of God into that soldier. It is not rocket science, it is just a simple fact.

The last aspect of our ministry is that my wife knows what it is like to be left behind and therefore is able to be an encouragement to many of the spouses of the soldiers we work with. Many think of the soldier who is deployed but few ever think about the family that is left behind. The wife of a soldier goes through a separation that most folks can never understand. So many of the wives of soldiers that we have met and spoken with identify with my wife as she shares some of the trials she went through during my deployment and after my return. Often they make comments like, "I thought I was the only one who felt that way," and it helps them to understand that they are not alone. The children also often have a difficult time understanding why dad and sometimes mom had to leave home for such a long time. We have materials that help these children understand that their dad or mom is serving our nation and the best thing they can do is not to complain, but to pray for their parents and just love them with all their hearts during and after their deployments. Children need to understand too that they can help their parents by being supportive and encouraging toward them during their deployments. We are here to offer that guidance and wisdom to those who will receive it.

ALLOWED TO LIVE

After two years of traveling away from my wife and home for months at a time several times a year, God finally worked on her heart that I needed her by my side. We began to pray for a vehicle to live in while we traveled out on the roads and gave God a simple shopping list. We asked him for a class "A" motor home that was in good mechanical order, well kept, and maintained. We did not care how old it was, simply that it was mechanically sound and big enough for us to comfortably live in day in and day out. While we were at a mission's conference, we shared our desire for such a vehicle and to our surprise we were told of just such a vehicle. Pastor Emeritus Everett Wilson of Vision Baptist Church took us just down the road from the church where there was a vehicle that fit our description to a "Tee". It looked so nice that in my heart I had already written it off as that we would never be able to afford it. The next day we went and talked to the man who owned it and found out that it was nearly twelve years old but only had eight thousand, two hundred twenty-two miles on it. The man who owned it was a retired bus mechanic who had purchased it with many upgrades so that he and his wife could travel once they both retired. Unfortunately, his wife became ill shortly after retirement and was not able to travel as they had planned. This broke his heart for several reasons but then the vehicle started to become a thorn in his side,

CHAPTER 12: OPERATION LIBERTY

reminding him of what he wanted to do but was now unable. This RV still blue-booked for over thirty-two thousand dollars and he was asking twenty-five thousand. However when he learned of why we wanted it and that we would be helping the military, he dropped the price down to twenty thousand dollars. Now I was interested and could see us affording such a vehicle. Two weeks later, after praying specifically about this one vehicle, we went back to take some pictures of it that we would use to try and raise the money to purchase it. While there, the owner asked me what price he had offered it to me for. I felt like I had been suckered in and now that I was interested in it he would explain why he needed more money. My heart sank as I repeated back to him the amount he had originally told me two weeks before. His response further confirmed my suspicions when he said, "Well, that will no longer do. So kind of upset, and with some sarcasm I am sure, I asked him, "Well then, what will do?" That is when he said, "I want you two to have this vehicle, even if you don't have the money right now. Just let me know that you want it and I will not sell it to anyone else. Even if they offer me more money I will call you and if you still want it, I will not sell it." Ok, that all sounded great to me but I still did not know what price he now wanted for the vehicle. Then he said, "Well, how about if I drop the price down to sixteen thousand, would that help you?" Can you imagine just how much my heart jumped for joy with that news! I told him, "Yes sir, we will take it" as we shook hands on the deal and went home to raise some money. A few months later we had raised enough to put two thousand down on it and found out that our credit union would finance it for us too. There was even enough left over to put new tires on it as the other ones were original and very badly weather-checked. Six days later I left town in this vehicle headed to Texas.

The trip to Texas was an eye opener into the world of living in an RV. We had never owned a vehicle like this before and knew little to nothing about how to maintain such a vehicle. Even though we both had CDL's this was something different. Besides all that, we had not driven it any further than from the man's home to our house and once to church so they could see how God blessed us. My wife was still working so I was still making this trip on my own. I left town with a half tank of fuel and twenty-six dollars in my pocket. I had spent all my travel money putting new tires on it once we realized that our car had bit the dust just a day before I was to leave town. That is also why I was driving to Texas in an RV by myself. Well, before heading to Texas I had several meetings in North Carolina, so that is the direction that I headed. This meant that I would have to charge any expenses on my

CHAPTER 12: OPERATION LIBERTY

credit card and pray that God would supply enough funds to pay for it all. Believing God wanted me to make this trip, I left home and headed south. As I was driving through Columbus, Ohio the left rear brake hung up and burned out on me. God directed me to a place where I could park for the night and then to a repair shop the next morning, which was a Saturday. Finding a shop open on Saturday that could handle a vehicle of that size was part of the problem but thankfully God directed and finally by nine A.M. I was directed to just such a shop. The repairs took several hours and after charging the cost of the repairs to my credit card, I was finally able to once again hit the road by twelve-thirty in the afternoon.

    Driving towards my destination it became dark, but still I had many miles to go. I cannot explain what was going through my mind as I went through the mountains for the first time with a vehicle of that size having just had my brakes worked on. I arrived at the church by early Sunday morning and just parked the vehicle and lay down to get some sleep. As I lay there I prayed, begging God to show me that this was His will. I was heavily in debt and had many more miles to go, so all I could see was a huge debt piling up and little if any funds to pay for it all. I lay there and wept before the Lord asking him for a miracle. I asked God if I had misunderstood His will for this trip or if I had misunderstood if I should have purchased this vehicle or not. I just needed to know that God was in this and this trip was His idea and not my own.

Later that morning I preached as I felt led of the Lord and God moved upon the hearts of the people. I never mentioned my need of funds, nor my indebtedness. I just trusted God and preached his infallible Word. I left that church in tears as they had given me an offering that paid off my credit card and left me with enough money to make the trip out to Texas.

> Matthew 6:31-34 *"Therefore take no thought, saying, What shall we eat? or, What shall we drink? or, Wherewithal shall we be clothed? (32) (For after all these things do the Gentiles seek:) for your heavenly Father knoweth that ye have need of all these things. (33) But seek ye first the kingdom of God, and his righteousness; and all these things shall be added unto you. (34) Take therefore no thought for the morrow: for the morrow shall take thought for the things of itself. Sufficient unto the day is the evil thereof."*

We have also seen our fair share of trials as we have begun to wholly follow the Lord. While out in Texas to present our ministry there, I received a phone call

CHAPTER 12: OPERATION LIBERTY

from my pastor. It was not uncommon for him to call me from time to time, but this time something was different. I could tell right away that something was bothering him and then he broke the news to me that after several years of trying to stay afloat and heading into winter with huge bills coming, he had suggested to the church that we close. I knew that we had been struggling financially because we had lost people for many reasons and the bad economy did not help any either. However, this was not anything I had seen coming. We had discussed selling our building and starting over in a store front and I was under the impression that was what was going to happen, so this phone call came as a huge shock to say the least. I was hurt and confused, and more than that, I no longer had a sending church, so I would have to cancel meetings and head home. That night as I prayed about the matter, God impressed upon my heart to speak with the pastor of the church where I was about what to do, so that is just what I did. I am so very thankful for this man of God who wept with me and prayed for me that afternoon. God then further impressed upon me to contact our only supporting church in Michigan (which was the same one that had shown us the RV) and explain to the pastor there what we were going through, so I did. I called and left him a message to call me and gave a brief description of what was going on. By the time he called me back he had already consulted with all the men of the church and offered to take us on as our sending church. When Pastor Cox called me back he said that as far as anyone there was concerned, we were now members of Vision Baptist Church and that I should not cancel meetings but just explain to them why we had a new sending church. We have become very fond of our new church and feel blessed that God directed us there. At the same time we are saddened by the fact that our church had to close, but we keep our former Pastor Dr. McCoy constantly in our prayers. He is still one of the most influential men in my life and will always be like a father to me. I love you Doc, and pray daily for God to bless you and your family.

That was just the first of many trips we would take in that RV and in February of two thousand eleven my wife handed in her resignation and just quit her job, joining me on the road. We had no idea of where the funds would come from to compensate for her income but trusted God that He would supply. Within just a few months God impressed upon several pastors' hearts to support our ministry. That means we went from just six percent of our needed monthly support to over twenty-five percent, which made up for most of my wife's income. God is so good all the time.

As of the publishing of this book, we have now been on the road together for just over 3 ½ years; living

CHAPTER 12: OPERATION LIBERTY

in our RV, trusting God to meet our needs, and enjoying life to the fullest. My wife and I both feel that we have never in our lives felt so free.

CHAPTER THIRTEEN

Tracts & Other Resources

In the following pages are three Gospel tracts that the Lord has allowed me to write. Each one written for a specific purpose, to address some of the reasons folks have given for why they don't believe they can or need to be saved. First however, let me start with information on Liberty Baptist Bible College. Although Liberty Baptist Church had to close its doors, the college was moved with us under the Authority of Vision Baptist Church. You can learn more about it by visiting our website:

www.CorrespondenceBibleCollege4U.org

We also have two websites for our Ministry:

www.EvangelistRussellKidman.com &

www.OperaionLibertyMinistry.org

Learn more about Vision Baptist Church at:

www.VisionBaptistChurchMI.com

Thank you for reading this book and we pray that it has been a blessing to you in some small way.

ALLOWED TO LIVE

Dear Friend,

   Will You Have Time For…

ONE…

LAST…

THOUGHT?

APRIL 17ᵀᴴ, 1979 3:20 P.M.
"MOTORCYCLE AND SEMI-TRUCK COLLIDE"
FOSTORIA REVIEW TIMES
THIS IS THE TRUE TESTIMONY OF
MISSIONARY / EVANGELIST
DR. RUSSELL L. KIDMAN

CHAPTER 13: TRACTS & OTHER RESOURCES

THE MESS:

My parents split up when I was about nine years old. My mom remarried to a man who promised the moon, yet delivered only one beating after another. When I was old enough and big enough to stick up for myself he left too. Now however my mother was upset with me for ruining her second marriage, so she left. At almost seventeen years of age I had to learn about economics, not in school but in life.

THE MUSTANG & MONEY:

I had no place to live, no job to speak of, no food, but I did have a car. That is exactly where I lived for almost a year. I did anything I could to make money! *(Anything legal that is. I could not afford to get into trouble and have the authorities find out that I was living on my own.)* I pumped gas, delivered pizza, delivered newspapers, even cleaned houses. At last I was promoted from delivering papers to printing press assistant, which paid enough to live on.

THE MOVES:

The next year I kept house and babysat in exchange for a room to sleep in. In just two short years I had moved five times, finally ending up at an athletic organization who had rooms to rent *(more like a dent in the wall with a bed in it!)* but at least it was warm and dry. That cannot be said for the other places I had been, especially for my car.

THE MOTORCYCLE:

My car by now had about run its course and was fast on its way to the grave. I needed another form of transportation. A car was out of the question because I could not afford the payments for anything which was reliable. I had always wanted a motorcycle, and found out that I could get one for only a fourth of my income, so I did. It was a beautiful 754 CBK to say the least. With a four-cylinder engine bolted beneath my legs, and only about 500 lbs. of bike weight to push, YEAH IT WAS FAST! In a very short time I was riding this bike just like the pros you see on TV. I could lay her down in a corner as good as the best of them, and even chased down a Ferrari, well for a little ways anyway.

THE MISTAKE:

I was now eighteen years old, strong, healthy, a senior in high school and would be graduating in just a little over two months. I had a new ride, and was on my way to take my new girl out for the evening. About halfway there I realized I had forgotten the ring she had given me, so I went back to get it. As I was leaving town the second time there was a very slow car in front of me so I whipped my bike right on

CHAPTER 13: TRACTS & OTHER RESOURCES

around them. I was now going about 50-MPH, and as I was passing them, a semi-truck pulled out onto the road heading the same direction. He was moving slow so I decided to pass him too. As I began to pass this big truck, he decided to turn left, again crossing my path of travel, as he turned into a local restaurant. The witnesses say that I jumped 20 feet into the air, over the truck, and tumbled to where I lay bleeding profusely. In just a fraction of a second my bike smashed into the truck.

Although brought up in church, taught about Christ as a child, and even baptized at age 14, my last conscious thought was:

I'M GOING TO HELL!!

At that moment I KNEW without a doubt that
GOD was real,
Death was real,
Hell was real, and
I was going to split it wide open.

THE MESSAGE:

If being good could save us, then we would have to be good all the time. Yet which one of us can truly say we have never lied or deceived anyone. The Word of God says in Romans 3:10 "*As it is written, There is none righteous, no, not one;"* Romans 3:23 *"For all have sinned, and come short of the glory of God;"*

If being religious could save us, then religion would be the answer. Right! Yet the world had religion when Christ said in Luke 19:10 *"For the Son of man is come to seek and to save that which was lost."*

If religion is not the way, what is? In John 14:6 says, *"Jesus saith unto him, I am the way, the truth, and the life: no man cometh unto the Father, but by me."*

Because sin, even just one sin, shows rebellion to God, thus causing us to be dead spiritually. Romans 5:12 *"Wherefore, as by one man sin entered into the world, and death by sin; and so death passed upon all men, for that all have sinned:"*

Because of sin, a sacrifice had to be made on our behalf by one who did not sin. Romans 5:8 *"But God commendeth his love toward us, in that, while we were yet sinners, Christ died for us."*

We must realize that sin delivers to us a wage. Romans 6:23a *"For the wages of sin is death;..."*

But Jesus Christ received that wage for all who will receive His free gift. Romans 6:23b *"...but the gift of God is eternal life through Jesus Christ our Lord."*

CHAPTER 13: TRACTS & OTHER RESOURCES

How then do we receive His free gift? Romans 10:9-10 *"That if thou shalt confess with thy mouth the Lord Jesus, and shalt believe in thine heart that God hath raised him from the dead, thou shalt be saved".* (10) *"For with the heart man believeth unto righteousness; and with the mouth confession is made unto salvation."*

ONE LAST THOUGHT:

Will you take the time to think about eternity? You may live for many years to come and that is what we all desire, but if you do not, and this is your last opportunity to receive Christ, take it while you still can. In Hebrews 10:31 God's Word says: *"It is a fearful thing to fall into the hands of the living God."*

Pray, repent to God of your sins, ask Him to save your soul and be your Saviour today. Here are two verses that show God has never turned anyone away.

John 3:16! *"For God so loved the World, that he gave His only begotten son, that Whosoever believeth on Him Shall not Perish, but have everlasting life."*

Romans 10:13 *"For whosoever shall call upon the name of the Lord shall be saved."*

After this experience I had to take one last thought. I decided to accept Jesus Christ as my Saviour. Will you do the same?

Please let us know of your decision by filling out the form below and mailing it to us, or visit our website and send us an E-mail (Subject: Born Again)

Romans 10:11 *"For the scripture saith, Whosoever believeth on Him shall not be ashamed."*

BATTLE READY SIR

ALLOWED TO LIVE

This was the Battle Cry of 2nd Battalion 29th Field Artillery as we prepared for Combat and were deployed to Desert Shield / Desert Storm in 1990-1991. We were...

BATTLE READY! HOOAH!

You and your unit have been chosen for whatever reason; that is not the question here. However, the question remains...

Are You Battle Ready?

It is not a question of whether or not you are physically or mentally fit for combat, but rather, are you prepared should the time come for you, like many soldiers before, who were called upon to give the ultimate sacrifice? If you are prepared for it you will not have to worry about it. In the meantime, consider the following questions:

If you died tonight would <u>YOU</u> go to Heaven?

Have you got the <u>Gift of GOD that is FREE</u>?

Isn't it funny how we all plan for our Future

But hardly ever plan for ETERNITY?

CHAPTER 13: TRACTS & OTHER RESOURCES

If you really want to be "Battle Ready," here is what you must understand: Most soldiers struggle through life because of what they had to do during combat, but understand that GOD, throughout history, used nations to judge other nations by the use of WAR.

Joshua 8:1 And the LORD said unto Joshua, Fear not, neither be thou dismayed: take all the people of war with thee, and arise, go up to Ai: see, I have given into thy hand the king of Ai, and his people, and his city, and his land:

and King David said:

Psalms 18:34 He teacheth my hands to war, so that a bow of steel is broken by mine arms.

Being a Soldier will of itself not keep you out of heaven but we have all told a lie at one time or another which proves we are all sinners in need of a Saviour.

Romans 3:23 For all have sinned, and come short of the glory of God;

Because of sin we must repent...

Acts 3:19 Repent ye therefore, and be converted, that your sins may be blotted out, when the times of refreshing shall come from the presence of the Lord;

We must believe on Jesus Christ...

ALLOWED TO LIVE

***John 1:12** But as many as received him, to them gave he power to become the sons of God, even to them that believe on his name:*

Now profess Jesus as Lord...

***Romans 10:9** That if thou shalt confess with thy mouth the Lord Jesus, and shalt believe in thine heart that God hath raised him from the dead, thou shalt be saved.*

You may live for many years to come and that is what we all desire, but if you do not, and this is your last opportunity to receive Christ, take it while you still can. In Hebrews 10:31 God's Word says: *"It is a fearful thing to fall into the hands of the living God."*

Pray, repent to God of your sins, ask Him to save your soul and be your Saviour today. Here are two verses that show God has never turned anyone away.

John 3:16! *"For God so loved the World, that he gave His only begotten son, that Whosoever believeth on Him Shall not Perish, but have everlasting life."*

Romans 10:13 *"For whosoever shall call upon the name of the Lord shall be saved."*

Will you now take time to think about Eternity?

CHAPTER 13: TRACTS & OTHER RESOURCES

Please visit our website to let us know of your decision by an E-mail (Subject: Born Again)

Romans 10:11"*For the scripture saith, Whosoever believeth on Him shall not be ashamed.*"

Dr. Russell Kidman, Ph.D.

Website: www.OperationLibertyMinistry.org

I'M SO CONFUSED!!!

HAVE YOU EVER WONDERED WHY THERE ARE SO MANY DIFFERENT BIBLES AND CHURCHES....

I CORINTHIANS 14:33
FOR GOD IS NOT THE AUTHOR OF CONFUSION, BUT OF PEACE, AS IN ALL CHURCHES OF THE SAINTS.

CHAPTER 13: TRACTS & OTHER RESOURCES

WHERE TO START?

Have you ever just been confused about anything at all? Have you ever had friends or family throw in their opinions only to cause you more confusion? At this point where do you turn or who do you turn too?

WHAT ABOUT THE BIBLE?

Does it really matter which "Bible" you use as long as you read it and obey it? Various books have been written to answer this question but today we want to look at it from a somewhat different direction.

WHICH TRANSLATION SHOULD YOU USE?

Are they all the Word of God? If so, then they should all say the same thing right? Yet we know that this is not true and is one of the leading causes of confusion in our churches today. One says that we must use the NIV, NKJV, RSV or NEV, and yet another says it is the KJV. Which is it? There are so many, is there really just one that is right? How do we know which argument is right? Let's look at what the Scriptures say in:

> Genesis 1:1-3 *In the beginning God created the heaven and the earth. 2 And the earth was without form, and void; and darkness was*

upon the face of the deep. And the Spirit of God moved upon the face of the waters. 3 And God said, Let there be light: and there was light.

Here in Genesis 1:1-3 we have the plurality of God the Father in all three verses. God the Holy Spirit in verse two and God the Son in the spoken word of verse three. To back this up let's look at *John 1:1-3 In the beginning was the Word, and the Word was with God, and the Word was God. 2 The same was in the beginning with God. 3 All things were made by him; and without him was not any thing made that was made.*

This should then make it clear that the Bible is God's written Word, which is God's very testimony of His spoken word, which according to Scripture is God the Son, Jesus Christ.

This begs us to ask the question, is there more than one Christ? Is there a different Jesus to fit all the different "Bibles" that are being printed today? Again we must look to Scripture for our answers.

Galatians 1:6-9 I marvel that ye are so soon removed from him that called you into the grace of Christ unto another gospel: 7 Which is not another; but there be some that trouble you, and would pervert the gospel of Christ. 8 But though we, or an angel from heaven,

CHAPTER 13: TRACTS & OTHER RESOURCES

preach any other gospel unto you than that which we have preached unto you, let him be accursed. 9 As we said before, so say I now again, If any man preach any other gospel unto you than that ye have received, let him be accursed.

Jesus, as well as the disciples, made it very clear to the early church that if anyone taught contrary to the teachings that He handed down to His disciples and the church, they were accursed. Therefore anyone who teaches that any bible will do is really teaching another Christ. This is where you are encouraged to do your own word study comparison and find out how the modern day translations remove the Deity of Christ, the Blood Sacrifice, Holiness from the disciples and angels, The Virgin Birth, and other doctrines taught by Jesus to His disciples. If Jesus is the Word of God then there can be only one written Word of God that is True and Faithful. There are so many other reasons for trusting the King James Bible as God's Preserved Word but space herein limits us. Please contact us for more information or books on this subject.

WHAT ABOUT THE CHURCH?

When I first was saved I did something that astonishes most Christians. I quit going to church. This was because I was raised in so many denominations throughout my life, each with different teachings that I figured the only way to find the truth was to stop listening to others, find the church in the Bible, and then search for a church like that. After studying and learning the doctrines of Jesus Christ, I began revisiting those denominations I was taken to as a child. Also during this studying I learned that almost all denominations were splits off of one "church" but there was one group that traced their heritage back to Jesus Christ and the disciples. With this new information it was not long before I found the church that Jesus Christ built.

After questioning His disciples about who He really was, Jesus declared the founding of His church.

Matthew 16:15-18 He saith unto them, But whom say ye that I am? 16 And Simon Peter answered and said, Thou art the Christ, the Son of the living God. 17 And Jesus answered and said unto him, Blessed art thou, Simon Barjona: for flesh and blood hath not revealed it unto thee, but my Father which is in heaven. 18 And I say also unto thee, That thou art Peter, and upon this rock I will build my church; and the gates of hell shall not prevail against it.

CHAPTER 13: TRACTS & OTHER RESOURCES

This Scripture is used to teach that Peter was the first pope of the universal church known today as Catholicism. However when you study out the words that Jesus used here you will find that the name Peter means pebble or small stone and we know from the prophets that Jesus is the Rock to which He referred.

Psalms 118:22 *The stone which the builders refused is become the head stone of the corner.*

Isaiah 28:16 *Therefore thus saith the Lord GOD, Behold, I lay in Zion for a foundation a stone, a tried stone, a precious corner stone, a sure foundation: he that believeth shall not make haste.*

Matthew 21:42 *Jesus saith unto them, Did ye never read in the scriptures, The stone which the builders rejected, the same is become the head of the corner: this is the Lord's doing, and it is marvellous in our eyes?*

This clearly teaches that Jesus is the "Stone" in Matthew 16:18 upon which He said He would build HIS Church, not a church, but HIS CHURCH.

Why is this important, well because if it is His Church then we can eliminate those that do not follow His Teachings and Doctrine.

To find the Church Founded and Headed by the Lord Jesus Christ all we must do is to read and study the Church of the New Testament.

There is a TRUE CHURCH and it is not universal nor is it invisible. The New Testament Church was a Visible Local Body of Born again Baptized Believers.

One is Born again by Repenting of your sin and asking Jesus Christ to Save your Soul. One becomes a Baptist by emersion in obedience to the Word of God. One is a Christian who lives like Jesus Christ lived.

So where are you today? Do you know Jesus as Saviour and Lord? Do you Trust in His Word? Are you in His Church? If you say you are a Christian, then do you live as Christ lived in obedience to His Father? If you would like help with these questions please feel free to visit or contact us at:

www.VisionBapitstChurchMI.com

ABOUT THE AUTHOR

Dr. Russell Kidman
And his wife Cathy
Founders of
Operation Liberty
Missionaries To
Our Military

Brother Kidman was deployed to Operation Desert Shield and Operation Desert Storm during the Liberation of Kuwait in 1990-1991. He was a sergeant serving as a Fire Direction NCO and secondary Chemical Specialist for Alpha Battery 2nd Battalion 29th Field Artillery Unit. He was deployed as General Support Reinforcement to 42nd Brigade and 3rd Armor Division.

Brother Kidman and his wife are now missionaries to our military with a firsthand understanding of what the soldier who is deployed and the family who is left behind are experiencing. Most people see the soldier coming home but fail to realize the struggles of returning home and readjusting to civilian life and family. This is where Brother Kidman applies his

ALLOWED TO LIVE

experience and knowledge of God's Word to help our soldiers and their families from a Biblical perspective.

GOD CALLED – These Are My Credentials

SALVATION - 8/2/1980

While visiting my Dad one year after I had a terrible motorcycle accident, under heavy conviction, I told him that I needed to be saved. Right then and right there he led me to the Lord. What a wonderful and merciful God to allow me to be saved.

CALLING - 2/28/1988

Just one year after I was saved I believe God placed His call upon my life but I did not respond until I was in the military in Baumholder, Germany attending Grace Baptist Church. During revival services I answered the call to preach the gospel of the Lord Jesus Christ. God gave me three years under Pastor Tim Clark's leadership as he grounded me in the Word of God.

YOUTH MINISTRY - 6/14/1992

Upon leaving the military, I was asked to be youth pastor at a Baptist Church in my wife's home town. Within just a few years God moved me into a full-time position in the Detroit area. For 13 years my wife and I served the Lord leading many young souls to Christ.

MISSIONARY/EVANGELIST - 7/2/2006

Who knows how long God has been planning this, but as for me it all started with a return trip back to Grace Baptist Church of Baumholder, Germany to provide special music for a men's retreat in May of 2006. I returned home with a greater burden for all those serving our country. God had opened my eyes to see a need in our Reserve and National Guard Units, their families and our Veterans. - Evangelism 11/3/2003

ABOUT THE AUTHOR

EDUCATION
Midwestern Baptist College ~ Pontiac, MI
   ~ Associates of Arts Biblical Studies
Liberty Baptist Bible College ~ Rochester Hills, MI
   ~ Bachelors of Arts Biblical Studies
Liberty Baptist Theological Seminary ~ Rochester Hills, MI
   ~Masters of Theology
   ~ Doctor of Theology
American Christian University ~ Gastonia, NC
   ~ Doctor of Philosophy

www.ingramcontent.com/pod-product-compliance
Lightning Source LLC
Chambersburg PA
CBHW060524100426
42743CB00009B/1423